# *Moura*

# MOURA

## *Her Autobiography*

*Moura Lympany*
*and*
*Margot Strickland*

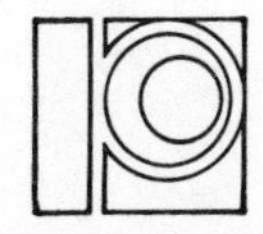

PETER OWEN
LONDON & CHESTER SPRINGS PA

PETER OWEN PUBLISHERS
73 Kenway Road London SW5 0RE
Peter Owen books are distributed in the USA by
Dufour Editions Inc. Chester Springs PA 19425–0449

First published in Great Britain 1991


ISBN 0–7206–0824–4

A catalogue record for this book is available
from the British Library

Printed in Great Britain by Billings of Worcester

# *Contents*

# *List of Illustrations*

# *Acknowledgements*

Many friends and colleagues have helped me with the preparation of my autobiography for publication. In particular I should like to thank the following: Mrs Peter Andry, Ms Andrée Back, Shirley, Lady Beecham, Mrs Maureen Bishop, Mr Fritz Curzon, Mme Hélène Galangau, M. Emil Gazeu, Graeme Kay, Mme J. Morilyon-Loysen, Sister Margaret Macdonald of Our Lady of Sion, Mrs Kenneth Sillito, Miss Joan Slater, Mrs Janet Snowman and the Library of the Royal Academy of Music, Peter Vansittart, John Whibley and Mrs Sylvia Witts.

The extract from the poem 'Racines' by Marcel Jourda on p. 142 is published by permission of the author.

If the artist gravely writes,
To sleep it will beguile.
If the artist gaily writes,
It is vulgar style.

If the artist writes at length,
How sad his hearer's lot!
If the artist briefly writes,
No man will care one jot!

If an artist simply writes,
A fool he's said to be.
If an artist deeply writes,
He's mad: 'tis plain to see.

In whatever way he writes,
He can't please every man:
Therefore let an artist write
How he likes and can!

*Felix Mendelssohn*, 1826

# 1

# Moura Johnstone

It is unfashionable to believe in the power of blood yet I have often wondered if Russian blood runs in my veins. My Austrian great-grandfather was a lawyer from Würzburg. Herr Kaupp was his name and when he was a young man he was pressured to serve with the Prussian Army, a prospect he found so hateful he ran away to England where, in Devon, he met an Irish girl and married her. Their daughter, Mrs Robert Limpenny, was my grandmother. She must have talked about the Russia her father had visited, and probably fired my mother with the desire to go there.

The Limpenny family were traditionally public-spirited: my great-grandfather was three times Mayor of Exeter and a window in Exeter Cathedral was his memorial from a devoted family and a grateful community. Earlier Limpennys (or Lympanys, as they then spelled it) were buried in the churchyard at Liskeard over the border in Cornwall. They could trace their descent from Edward I[1] but they had become impoverished and of necessity had gone into trade. At one time they had been quite successful and had owned three shops in Plymouth selling sports equipment, but during my mother's girlhood these had dwindled to

---

[1]A Denise Lympany was the eighth great-granddaughter of Edward I.

one, in George Street.[2] There were five daughters and two sons in the family. The two sons, Charles and Freddie, were worshipped; everything was sacrificed to ensure their prosperous futures. Charles went to Dartmouth to become a cadet in the Royal Navy[3] while Freddie joined the British American Tobacco Company and went to the Argentine, where he became director. The only future for the five sisters – Beatrice, Mina, Frances, Ernestine,[4] Madge[5] – was to sit at home and wait for a husband to come along. Till then they had to fend for themselves. Frances, who was clever, started a school in Plymouth; Mina, who was beautiful and devoted to her mother, stayed at home; but my mother, Beatrice, was too spirited to languish in Devon. She taught herself languages and music, and at the earliest opportunity took the long train journey across Eastern Europe to Russia, where she had obtained a post teaching English.

The reality of life in Russia transcended the tales Beatrice had heard in her youth. St Petersburg in the years before the First World War was brilliant – for some. It was a society of magnificent assemblies presided over by the Tsar, the Tsarina and the imperial court at the Winter Palace built by Peter the Great in 1703 on the banks of the River Neva. My mother had come to St Petersburg from a provincial seaside town, one of many Englishwomen who had literally educated the world. The imperial nurseries were dominated by English nannies. Beatrice had a passion for learning and a vocation for teaching. Her pupils were the three daughters of the wealthy banking Benenson family: Manya,[6] Flora,[7] and Fira.[8]

Beatrice Limpenny was conscientious and energetic, and set about her tasks so endearingly the Benensons made a

---

[2]Now demolished.
[3]Rear-Admiral Charles Limpenny, DSO.
[4]Ernestine was married and widowed three times.
[5]Madge married an Australian.
[6]Manya translated *Boris Pasternak: An Essay in Autobiography* (Collins Harvill, 1959).
[7]Flora worked for Marks & Spencer and published an autobiography.
[8]Fira went to the United States, where she established her own couture house.

great pet of her. She was never treated as a menial but as a member of the family, whom she accompanied to the opera and the ballet as a matter of course. There were parties galore: skating parties in winter when the temperature was below freezing for many months of the year. It was magical, skating along the many inlets and waterways that criss-crossed the River Neva, strung together with innumerable bridges, and on the banks in the cold light glittered golden spires and cupolas among the pastel-coloured buildings. It was a dream city, described as 'music set in stone'.

The society to which the Benensons introduced my mother was worldly, elegant and cultured, in sparkling contrast to her restricted social circle in Plymouth. She enthusiastically embraced everything Russian: the language, the literature and, above all, the music, for which she conceived a passion that was to last all her life. The Benensons constantly begged her not to practise so much at the piano they had put in her room. So happy was my mother in this milieu far from home that she persuaded her sisters, Mina and Frances, to join her in St Petersburg, with equally happy results. They taught the entire aristocracy and were well rewarded by their employers.

At the height of the First World War, in 1915, London was thronged with troops being sent off to the trenches in France. Many did not return. Those who did, were shell-shocked, gassed, wounded. Tommies in their hospital blue sang songs (like 'Keep the Home Fires Burning' by Ivor Novello) among the well-tended flower-beds in Hyde Park, thankful to be alive and away from the horror of the front. At 1 Hyde Park Gate, across the Bayswater Road, Lady Hamilton (daughter of the Dowager Marchioness of Deanston) with her helpers sorted out the gifts that poured in in response to her appeal for khaki shirts, socks, writing-paper, Woodbine cigarettes and tins of condensed milk, to send to the troops fighting under her husband, General Sir Ian Hamilton's command in the Dardanelles. Half-way down Park Lane at Grosvenor House, Lady Townsend had instigated the popular recreation of afternoon teas for officers. The men in tailored khaki uniforms, polished Sam Browne belts and shoes, and naval officers in dark-blue serge, brass buttons and gold braid, sipped fragrant tea from porcelain cups, and nibbled sandwiches and home-made cakes. Accompanying the tinkling of the china and the genial chatter of the men was a petite lady playing a darkly polished grand piano raised upon a dais. When she had finished her piece, polite applause greeted her performance. She bowed, slipped an opulent white fur coat over her shoulders, and left the stage. Beatrice Limpenny had come home from Russia. The white fur coat was a farewell gift from the Benenson family. She was now thirty-five.

Among the audience one day was a tall, handsome officer, also aged thirty-five, one of a contingent of Australians in London who had fought in the Dardanelles, covered himself with medals, and was now on a well-earned leave. He was not, however, an Australian himself, but English. He had run away from home and school in his teens and joined the Army as a private, was 'bought out' by his father, and escaped a second time, making sure he would not be so easily recaptured by boarding a ship to Australia. He dreamed of buying a farm, fell into the hands of unscrupulous money-lenders, lost all he had, together with his expectations under his grandfather's will, and worked as a labourer. On the outbreak of war, he joined the Australian forces and was duly commissioned a captain. His name was Captain John Johnstone.

Beatrice was a resourceful, practical, intelligent and versatile woman who had earned her living from an early age. By the time she met John Johnstone she could speak, read and write seven languages and she had a business brain too. She had wisely invested her savings in private houses in Devon, living in one and renting out the other two. She was by this time longing to marry, chiefly because she yearned for a child. 'If I don't marry soon,' she declared to an astonished friend, 'I shall have an illegitimate baby!'

This was unlikely, since she came of a most correct, prudish, devout Roman Catholic family.

Captain Johnstone was the fifth child and second surviving son of Dr John Johnstone Salcombe Johnstone of the village of Sandhurst, just outside Gloucester. He had been educated at the Benedictine Ampleforth College in Yorkshire. He was one of thirteen orphaned children who were proud of their family's history. They were of the clan Johnstone of Annandale, insistent that their surname should be spelled with a t and an e. Charles II had created the earldom of Annandale in 1662 in Dumfriesshire. Several of John Johnstone's forbears had spent fortunes trying to prove they were the rightful heir to the extinct earldom of Annandale but had failed.[9] John Johnstone's elder brother Bede[10] was a commanding figure with a striking Wellington nose and a monocle; after training at Sandhurst he was launched on a distinguished military career. He had married into a family from Leamington Spa. John himself was charming, reckless and feckless. He was an adventurer, and although he walked tall and had a princely manner, he had nothing behind him but his name and background; he would sell anything he was given for ready cash with which to get through the day. He had no thought for the morrow. His grandfather, Dr George Johnstone of Ecclefechan and Edinburgh University, had come to Gloucestershire from Scotland, fallen in love with an heiress, Mary Salcombe, and married her.

In her white fur coat Beatrice must have looked rich, and John Johnstone embarked upon a rapid courtship. By the time he met Beatrice, he was something of a Don Juan, and Beatrice was soon mesmerized by his charm and fell in love with him. Did she propose to him? He warned her that he was a good-for-nothing and had no money, but she replied that it did not matter as she owned three houses. He

---

[9]In 1985 the earldom was revived by Patrick Hope-Johnstone, Earl of Annandale and Hartfell.

[10]Lt-Colonel Bede Johnstone, DSO, Indian Army.

cautioned her that he was not made for marriage, but she brushed all his protestations aside, and together they went to Devon to meet the Limpenny family, and then to Bristol to meet what was left of the Johnstones.[11] John's mother, Gertrude, and father, had died, and the younger children were cared for by a hated housekeeper. That was why John had run away from home. Their uncle and guardian, Vincent Mather,[12] from Manchester, met John and his fiancée Beatrice on one of John's leaves from the front.

John and Beatrice were soon married and set up home in one of Beatrice's three houses at 10 Barnpark, Teignmouth, before John rejoined his regiment and returned to the trenches in France.

On 18 August of the following year, 1916, at one of Beatrice's other houses, at Saltash, their first child and only daughter was born, two weeks earlier than expected. When it came to choosing a name for me, my parents had only one choice: Moura. John's grandmother had been Mary Salcombe of Gloucester, and his mother was called Gertrude. Therefore on the birth certificate I was registered as Mary Gertrude Johnstone. But from the moment of my birth, as my mother had vowed, from her love for Russia, I was always called Moura, the Russian version of Mary.

I was born under the astrological sign of Leo the Lion. I was very strong and throve with extraordinary speed. I was also hypersensitive and easily startled by sudden noises, felt the slightest change in temperature, and was terrified of dogs, horses, the dark and ghosts. When I was nine weeks old my mother wrote to her Aunt Susie, from 4 Atlantic Road, Newquay:

> I am so pleased to say that my darling babe is growing well . . . the weather continues so beautiful and we can

---

[11]Ethelreda, Wulstan, William, Winifred, Hilda, Margaret, Helen and Ursula.

[12]Sir William Mather, MP, was an industrialist and Russian scholar.

sit out every afternoon by the beach. We had to go to the doctor's about the vaccination, and his wife said she never saw a baby at Moura's age so intelligent as she laughs and tries to speak. . . . Nurse declares she will be teething in a week or so . . . she goes regularly to Church and one of the Nuns stopped me and said I was spoken of as an example to Mothers for bringing their babies to Church!

Teignmouth was a delightful place for small children to grow up in. The Devon air was soft and balmy, as gentle as the sea-waves lapping the sheltered southern shores. Further inland Dartmoor with its mystical atmosphere and grey-brown wild ponies provided an ever-present magnet for excursions and rambles.

My grandmother spoiled me. She lived at 10 Carlisle Terrace, Plymouth, and I was often at her house to be treated to all the Devonshire specialities: crab soup and clotted cream and scones, which I devoured with a hearty appetite. The Hoe was a vital element in stimulating my imagination with tales of Sir Francis Drake, Queen Elizabeth I and the great battle of the Spanish Armada.

Uncle Charlie and his wife were better off than we were. My beautiful cousins Peggy[13] and Pat[14] were older than I was and seemed like creatures from another planet. They attended expensive boarding-schools and were later presented at court. I was never envious of them. I always accepted the fact that they had everything of the best because their father had a very good position, whereas my father had not. That was how life was. What I was best at, from an early age, was playing the piano. My mother taught me my right-hand notes. Quite young I played with some force, trying to get more out of that little old parlour upright piano

[13]Peggy married Lt-Colonel Farquharson, Indian Army.
[14]Pat married Cecil Orr, director of the AA.

of my mother's than it was able to give. I was trying, not to play loudly but to make a more effective sound than my small body could manage. At the age of six, all I cared about was my doll and my piano. I tried to compose tunes too.

'She thumps!' complained my father when he came home on leave. Once, when my mother was trying to teach me to dance the Dying Swan, which she had seen Pavlova dance in St Petersburg, he came into the room as I was fluttering my hands as prettily as I could, and remarked: 'Moura dances like a cow!'

When the war was over and the Armistice declared, my father was at home all the time, and unemployed. After all his adventures overseas and the excitement of battle and the glory of uniform and the medals, he found domesticity stifling. He resorted to selling insurance for Sun Life of Canada. He was not good at selling insurance, but earned enough for him to continue. With the idea of selling insurance to the members, he joined the local golf-club, spending long hours on the links followed by even longer spells at the nineteenth hole. He had a real talent for the game and won many silver cups and trophies, but he quickly sold them for ready cash.

My mother, ever industrious, taught the cello, the piano, Russian, German, and French. She tramped about all over the place to earn a few shillings. It hurt me and still does to think of how hard she worked for us. She ran the house with the help of a young French girl, an early au pair who wanted to learn English. She spoke only French to me, which is why I learned to speak French before I could speak English.

When I was four years old my brother Anthony was born, and two years later Joseph. I adored them and loved helping my mother and the French girl look after them. My mother was so often working I was like a mother to them myself, bathing them, dressing them, feeding them, playing with them and teaching them. Tony was tall, fair, handsome, lively; Joseph was the image of my father, beautiful, but serious and honourable.

My mother was deeply mortified by my father's incessant sponging. He would beg from anybody and everybody he met. From his generous elder brother Bede he would cadge an overcoat, gloves, a cane, and at once sell them. My mother confided to me that she dreaded his meeting her friends on account of this embarrassing behaviour. He was shameless. Why did she not leave him? I asked. 'Oh, but I had three beautiful children!' she replied. The truth was that she loved him.

But as we children grew and the depressing twenties progressed she worried constantly as to how she was going to educate three children. Her brothers offered help financially with the boys' education. But what about me?

As a good Catholic my mother read the periodical *The Catholic Times* and one day the solution seemed to present itself when she saw advertised in its pages a convent boarding-school for girls in Belgium whose fees were £5 a term. Almost without hesitation, she had written to the convent, I had been accepted, and with a label tied to my coat buttonhole proclaiming who I was and my destination, during the Easter holidays in 1922 when I was six years old my mother and I boarded the train for Dover, I was put on the boat bound for Ostend, and waved a sad goodbye to my mother.

I already spoke French fluently which helped me on the journey, and I was not frightened of travelling the relatively short distance by sea on my own. I had never been away from my mother and little brothers and had never gone anywhere beyond Plymouth, but when one is a child one accepts what is one's lot. I did just as I was told. I was a stout little girl and had been taught good manners by my mother. And although when the boat put to sea the grey waves rose and fell ominously and the boat rocked alarmingly, causing my stomach to heave, I clamped my mouth shut. I was not and never have been seasick.

When I arrived at Ostend, among the many persons crowding the decks I was confronted by a middle-aged man who announced himself as Monsieur Aurez, the brother of Soeur Léonarda of the Convent des Soeurs de Marie at Tongres (Tongeren), in the Limbourg Province, the school where I was to be a pupil. Monsieur Aurez took me by the hand and led me to the train for Brussels: 54 Avenue du Vert-Chasseur, Uccle (a suburb of Brussels), was his address. I was amazed at the luxury of his house. I had never seen anywhere like it in my short life. Monsieur Aurez was the richest member of a large family of jewellers, whose premises were in the Boulevard Adolphe Max. The other members of the family lived almost next door to each other and were all jewellers, in the Rue au Beurre, just off the Grande Place, whose façades glittered with gold in the spring sunshine, dazzling my eyes. Madame Dalmotte lived at 28, and her sister-in-law Madame Miévis at 32, and her sister-in-law, also Madame Miévis, at 44. I at once made friends with Suzanne Aurez and Jeanne Miévis, her cousin, and their parents made 'la petite anglaise' most welcome. I was overwhelmed with kindness and love.

I was neither homesick nor lonely in the comfortable embrace of these four friendly families. They treated me as one of their children, and their children treated me as a sister. I loved them and they loved me. I was an affectionate little girl and they were demonstrative. When I left the house, say, number 28, to go to number 44 Rue au Beurre, even for a short while, I would kiss Madame Dalmotte goodbye. On my return, kisses were exchanged once more in greeting. And it was just the same when I arrived and left the family Miévis at number 44. These were not empty, superficial formalities. I felt completely secure in their real love and care for me.

There was a piano in the dining-room of number 32 Rue au Beurre and I was always sitting at it, practising the scales and short exercises my mother had taught me, and making up tunes of my own. During meals, when I had finished one course, I would glance longingly at the piano and ask: 'Puis-je aller jouer?' The family readily gave me permission and would good-naturedly continue with their meal accompanied by my playing.

My mother had already decided that the piano was to be my career, but she told the school she wanted me to learn the harp or the violin too. 'You will never earn your living playing the piano!' she warned me. A harpist or violinist could usually find employment in an orchestra.

The Easter holidays over, Jeanne, Suzanne and I went to the Convent at Tongres, the oldest town in Belgium, dominated by the statue of the great national hero Ambiorix. Soeur Léonarda, Monsieur Aurez's sister, took charge of me. I was excused most of the ordinary school curriculum in favour of the piano and the violin. My first piano teacher, known to everybody as 'Miss', was strange to relate an Englishwoman. I never knew her name. I got on by leaps and bounds even though, when I was taught the left-hand notes and some primary works for two hands, I protested: 'I shall never be able to play different notes in different hands!'

I loved practising the piano, and it is thanks to the nuns that I got on so well with my music. They realized I had an uncommon gift and did everything to help me. For instance, every evening from five to seven o'clock was study time for the girls, but I was allowed to practise instead. At these times I would take the other girls' sheet music from the shelf where it was kept, and sight-read everything I could get hold of. At examination times Soeur Léonarda would give me the chapter of history and literature from which the questions were set. I read them and I nearly always came first! The fact was I had a good memory and learned very quickly. I had an avidity to learn, a great thirst for knowledge and a curiosity about everything.

The piano examinations took place before the Jury Central in Liège, about an hour's journey from Tongres. I was never nervous of them and passed them easily, but the violin examinations were a different matter. I did not like learning the violin, had no aptitude for it, and when in the music-room for violin practice played instead the piano accompaniments. But I had no problems passing the piano examinations.

It soon got round the Convent and the town that there was this little English girl who played the piano very well. One of the visiting masters at the Convent was a Monsieur Edmond Jaminé, an erudite man of means, a retired lawyer, a poet, dramatist, musician and composer, now in his seventies. He came to the Convent to teach the girls drama. He was astounded when he heard me play, and I often played for him alone. 'Darling Bonpapa,' I called him. I was pressed into service to play for gymnastics, or to accompany the choir, or the play under rehearsal. It was never a chore and I loved it.

By the time I was nine years old I was practising five hours a day of my own volition, far too much for a small girl, and I began to suffer from migraines. I played alone in the Convent's Grande Salle. In the summer the nuns would try to get me away from the piano into the sunshine, but I could not be torn away from the piano. Once I was playing all one hot afternoon when I heard a noise at the window in front of me. I jumped off the piano-stool and ran to look out but could see nothing and nobody. Back to the piano I went and continued practising. Again I heard the noise at the window, as if stones were being thrown up at the glass panes. I looked round me for the first time and, aware of the awesome giant space of the Grande Salle behind me, suddenly became frightened and rushed out into the garden to find the dear nuns laughing and hiding from me. They had lured me out into the sunshine at last!

'Bach, Bach, and again Bach,' Rubinstein used to say. From the age of seven I was playing Bach – the two-part inventions and so forth, and always moving on to something more difficult, until I could play all the forty-eight preludes and fugues. By the time I was nine years old I had passed all my piano examinations and my English 'Miss' had been succeeded by a Belgian 'Madame'. One day she played us a piece of music which fascinated me, telling us that the student who passed her academic examinations with the highest marks would be allowed to study it next. I was determined to study that piece. I won and I did. It was Liszt's Polonaise in E Major. I was nine and a half. Monsieur Jaminé was so proud of me he commissioned a plaster cast of my right hand to be made and presented it to me to keep for posterity.

And now I was taken by a nun twice a month for special extra lessons with Professor Jules Debefve of the Conservatoire of Liège. These were paid for by my dear family of jewellers in Brussels with whom I spent my school holidays. Their generosity and kindness were endless. Madame Dalmotte bought me good clothes and, as she loved to sew, she made me beautiful silk dresses by hand, trimmed with Brussels lace.

The lessons in Liège were very exciting occasions for me. After the journey from Tongres, one of the nuns who had escorted me would take me to the Patisserie Bott where we would drink coffee and feast on the delectable pastries for which they were famous, before going to the Conservatoire.

Professor Debefve was an excellent tutor. He had composed and published a book of exercises, and he started me on my first really substantial work: the Mendelssohn Piano Concerto in G Minor.

About this time there was to be a great celebration in Tongres: the 700th anniversary of La Vierge Noire, the Black Virgin. Queen Elisabeth of Belgium was to visit the Convent. Monsieur Jaminé composed a special song, 'Onze Klockies' ('Our Little Bells'), for the choir to sing to Her Majesty. It was suggested that 'la petite anglaise' should also play a solo for the Queen. Of course I had read about kings and queens but they had little reality for me, inhabiting some sort of fairyland, and I could hardly believe that I was to play the piano for a real queen. I was very excited at the prospect and practised even harder, morning, noon and night, ignoring the painful migraines that beset me.

Madame Dalmotte arranged for my best pink silk dress, black patent-leather shoes and white silk socks to be sent out to the Convent, with pink silk ribbons to be tied round my fine, long, plaited hair. My front teeth had grown slightly crooked and crossed one over the other. However, as I was always laughing and smiling from high spirits and *joie de vivre*, there was no hiding them.

The day before the great occasion I was summoned by the Reverend Mother to her study. I would not be playing for the Queen after all, she told me, adding gently: 'It might turn the head of one so young.' The choir was to sing in procession through the streets of the town while four boys, dressed as pages, would carry two poles on their shoulders, from which hung two large brass bells. Wearing a long white dress and a white bandeau round my head, I would be allowed to strike first one bell, then the second bell, in accompaniment.

Thus early did I learn from the nuns of Tongres a valuable lesson in humility.

# 2

# Two Plaits and a Symphony Orchestra

My life in Belgium was so happy. I loved my school, I loved my work, I loved everyone, and everyone loved me. Four years passed and then the bomb fell. I spent most of the holidays with the Brussels families, as the expenses of travelling to England would have been too much for my mother. But on one of my rare visits to England my Uncle Charles was surprised at how foreign I had become. I was an English girl but I could hardly speak English and in every way was Belgian. He told my mother that she ought to bring me back to England.

The announcement that I was to be taken away from the Convent was greeted with tears and consternation, from me, my friends the nuns, and the kindly families in Brussels. Dolefully my things were packed, and then I was taken to London.

At one period of her life my mother had taught at the Convent School of Our Lady of Sion, in Chepstow Villas, near the Bayswater Road, London. They had loved her there, and so agreed to take me as a boarder at very reduced fees.

It was a great joy when my mother and I were invited to luncheon with my Aunt Dorrie and my cousins Peggy and Pat in their London flat in South Kensington. I was very excited, longing to meet again my beautiful cousins with whom I was sure I would make great friends, and I arrived from Belgium a most affectionate child. When we reached their flat where my cousins and aunt awaited us, I rushed up to them in turn and planted kisses on both of each of their cheeks in the Belgian manner. They were astonished by my unreserved behaviour; at that time displays of affection were 'not done' in England.

After luncheon my aunt led the way to her bedroom where, assembled on the bed, was a selection of clothes which they were going to give my mother and me. We were most grateful and left heaped with carrier bags filled with lovely things we could never have afforded to buy. I doubt whether my mother ever bought herself anything.

Our Lady of Sion had been founded by Theodore Rattisbone. Born in Strasbourg in 1807, he was converted to Roman Catholicism and ordained as a priest in 1830. His mission was to bring about greater understanding between Jews and Christians. The lovely wide corridors of the grand house in Chepstow Villas, off the Bayswater Road, were populated by nuns dressed in voluminous black habits with black veils floating from stiff, white bandeaux round their heads and chins. The girls wore black pleated skirts, stockings, bodices, shoes, relieved by starched white collars and cuffs, and, according to our forms, a coloured belt: red, yellow, green, violet and blue.

From my school in a little provincial Belgian town where I had been loved, spoiled, *gâtée*, I suddenly found myself a boarder in what seemed to me a huge building in a capital city, among hundreds of strange girls. I endured the first term in silence.

When the time came for me to return to Our Lady of Sion after the holidays, my mother and I were going up in the lift at Notting Hill Underground Station, when suddenly something gave way inside me. I jumped up and down in the lift, screaming: 'I *won't* go back! I will *not* go back!'

My mother had a very difficult time calming me down. I had to go back to the Convent, and gradually settled down to work.

The Convent had an unusual system of marking. Part of the founder's educational creed was the absence of the prefect system. Pupils' marks were to be awarded by them according to their consciences. This was to encourage and teach the girls honesty. Partly because I was unhappy, I suppose, on one occasion, whose details I cannot recall, I gave myself higher marks than I deserved. Of course I was found out and reported to Mother Paula, who instructed me to stay behind after lessons were over and the other pupils had gone. I received a long sermon from Mother Paula about honesty, and it must have had a profound effect upon me, because ever since I have found it very difficult not to tell the truth, however disagreeable and undiplomatic. I have often gone to the other extreme and been tactless and too outspoken, which sometimes offends. Honesty in one's work is essential for an artist and in this regard Mother Paula's lecture was another valuable lesson taught me by the nuns.

My brothers were now away at prep school, also in Belgium, and my mother rented a flat at Bexhill-on-Sea in Sussex, where I spent the school holidays.

Partly because I was still homesick for the Belgium I had loved so dearly, my mother also found a cheap holiday house in a tiny village on the Belgian coast near Westende, called Lombartzyde. It was only a half-hour's journey on the tram from the coast at Ostend. It was heaven for me to be back in Belgium, speaking French again, to play with my brothers, now grown much taller than I, and almost strangers. But not for long. We were a very close family, although developing in such different ways. Joseph was, even so young, religious, while Tony was reckless and loved danger.

We had a ten-minute walk to the beach at Lombartzyde where our favourite pastime was digging the wet, ribbed sand after the tide had gone out, and prising succulent mussels from the rocks. We would fill our pails with them and haul them back to the cottage for our mother to boil for our supper. We would crowd round the small stove and watch the black, barnacled shells open in the simmering water. They were delicious.

There was no piano at the rented house, so as my mother was determined I should not forgo my practising, she arranged for me to go and practise daily on the rickety little upright piano at the local café. The owner decided to arrange a concert. He asked a soprano to sing, I was asked to play the piano, and the local newspaper was invited to attend and report this unusual event in the little seaside resort. My mother, brothers and even my father all sat at small tables listening to the soprano trilling her high notes when a young man at the next table with a notebook on his knee and a pencil in his hand, leaned over towards me confidentially. 'She's awful!' he whispered. He was the newspaper reporter.

The soprano finished her song and it was my turn next. I cannot recall what I played, but when I finished and bowed, I rejoined my family and he had gone. The following day I rushed out to the local shop to buy a newspaper and scoured the pages. To my amazement I read an ecstatic paragraph about the singer. I decided then that I would not always believe what critics wrote!

Not far away from Lombartzyde was Le Coq, where there was an excellent golf-course, a magnet as far as my father was concerned. On the links at Le Coq my father met a young Hungarian, a golf enthusiast on holiday with his wife. They played together every day and became great friends. At the end of the holidays the young Hungarian was so impressed with my father and his prowess at golf that he invited him to be his guest in Hungary to teach him the game and advise on the laying out of a golf-course on his estate. The salary was to be five pounds a week and my father and mother would be honoured guests at the castle of Count Laszlo Karolyi – for this was the name of my father's golfing partner.

This extraordinary state of affairs was manna from heaven for my parents, always scraping along as best they could. My father could not refuse such a munificent offer from one of the greatest aristocratic families in Hungary. He casually accepted the invitation and when we three children were back at school in the autumn, my parents took the train to Budapest and the Karolyi estate outside the capital.

When my Uncle Charlie, now Rear-Admiral Limpenny, came home on leave, I was invited again to their London flat and, having been at the Convent of Our Lady of Sion for some time, I had grown more reserved in my manner. But I still spoke English with a foreign accent. 'Why can't she be like the other English girls?' he asked my mother. 'Riding, and so on?' He offered to pay for half a dozen lessons for me at a riding-school in Wimbledon. The charge was two and a half guineas. My cousins of course rode beautifully and even hunted, but I had never been on a horse in my life. My aunt lent me jodhpurs, boots and a hacking-jacket, together with a hard hat outgrown by my cousins, and off to Wimbledon I went for my first riding lesson.

It was the most terrible ordeal for me. First of all I was terrified of this huge animal, quiet old hack though it may have been. And when I was sitting on it, helped by the instructress, I was even more terrified to find myself so high up on a moving creature that took no notice when I tugged at the reins. I sat rigid with fright like a pole for five lessons – I never took the sixth.

After this episode I think my uncle gave up hope of his niece ever becoming the conventional English teenager he wished for.

During my second year at the Convent of Our Lady of Sion I began to enjoy hockey and tennis. When we were set an essay to write with the title 'My Hero', I chose Beethoven. Meanwhile glowing letters arrived for me almost every day from my mother in Hungary. It was the highlight of her life. She and my father were so happy; he playing golf every day with the Count and planning with him the layout of the golf-course, while my mother revelled in the countryside, the music and the art of Budapest. Both my parents were deeply appreciated by their hosts and their families.

All this time I had been studying the piano out of

school hours with an old friend of my mother's, Professor Ambrose Coviello. With him I worked on the Grieg Piano Concerto and he recommended that I enter for the Ada Lewis Scholarship at the Royal Academy of Music where he himself had been a student and then a professor. I would have worked hard at my studies anyway but now I had a goal to spur me to success. It was 1929 when I sat for the scholarship at the Royal Academy of Music in the Marylebone Road. The result would not be known until August. Meanwhile when the term ended I went to join my mother in Bexhill for the summer holidays.

Along the coast not far from Bexhill was the old fishing port of Hastings and its other half, St Leonards-on-Sea. Byron and his sister had spent a holiday in the fishing quarter and the Duke of Wellington his honeymoon. Decimus Burton the architect had designed much of St Leonards, but the twin towns had never attained the glamour and celebrity of Brighton. There was great competition among the seaside resorts to attract holiday-makers, and the powers that be at Hastings and St Leonards decided that what was needed was a splendid new concert hall to attract visitors. It was to be built where the towns met; some attractive public gardens had been created above an outcrop of natural rock, the White Rock.

The White Rock Pavilion at Hastings was soon opened and launched with great éclat, drawing all the noted musicians of the day and devoted audiences. The well-known conductor Basil Cameron appeared weekly during the season, and when my mother heard that a boy prodigy was to play the piano at one of the concerts at the Pavilion, she obtained tickets for herself and me.

The Pavilion faced the sea, sun and promenade. So far in my life I had practised and practised and I had sat for many examinations and passed all of them, musical and scholastic. But I had never attended a single concert. The excitement and anticipation of sitting in the audience that summer's afternoon at Hastings is something I shall never forget. I have no recollection of the programme but was deeply impressed by Cameron, an elegantly garbed figure in white tie and tails, baton in hand. The boy soloist's name I have long forgotten. I have related how the nuns at Tongres had taught me humility and the nuns in London honesty. In the interval I turned to my mother. 'Oh Mummy!' I cried. 'Couldn't I play with the orchestra?'

So when we returned to Bexhill my mother composed a letter to the conductor. To our surprise Mr Cameron replied that he would be prepared to hear me play, naming a date and time, at the White Rock Pavilion. For this crucial audition I played the Mendelssohn G Minor Piano Concerto. Mr Cameron was agreeably surprised and told us he would be delighted if I would play with his orchestra, but the soloists for the concert season at Hastings were already engaged. Would I play at Harrogate on 8 August?

8 August? That was ten days before my thirteenth birthday. We joyfully agreed.

What would I play? Mr Cameron asked. The only concerto I had memorized was the Mendelssohn in G Minor which I had studied with Jules Debefve at Liège and had just played. Mr Cameron suggested that I should therefore play this work. Then he turned to my mother. 'What is her full name?' he asked.

'Moura Johnstone,' she replied.

'Moura is a good concert name,' commented Mr Cameron thoughtfully. 'But Johnstone does not go with it.' I suppose he meant that Moura sounded like the kind of romantic and exotic name beloved by concert-goers, while Johnstone sounded too prosaic. 'What is your maiden name?' he asked my mother.

'Limpenny,' answered my mother, stressing the first syllable.

'A bit better,' remarked the conductor, repeating the name, savouring the sound. He still seemed dissatisfied.

'What about the old spelling,' my mother suggested helpfully. 'It is LYMPANY.'

'Perfect!' exclaimed Basil Cameron.

So in a few moments I became Moura Lympany, and I have remained Moura Lympany all my life.

At that time it was believed impossible for an Englishman or Englishwoman to succeed in the world of classical music or ballet without assuming a foreign name. Families of budding soloists held conferences with agents and impresarios to invent a new name for the artist. Thus Sarah Nelson the cellist became Zara Nelsova, Peggy Hookham became Margot Fonteyn, Lilian Alicia Marks was transformed by Diaghilev into Alicia Markova. There was no need for me to pretend: my slight foreign accent was genuine, and so was my name – but I was an English girl.

Everybody loved the name Moura Lympany – except my Johnstone nun-aunts, who feared the loss of my father's name Johnstone might suggest that I was illegitimate.

I could hardly believe that I was to play with a real orchestra under a well-known conductor. It was an extraordinary development and the concert at Harrogate was not far away. All my energies were now directed to preparing for this most vital début. The fee was to be five guineas, which would cover the train fares, hotel and all expenses. My unmarried Aunt Frances was to travel with my mother and me to Harrogate, and while I got on with my practising there were endless discussions as to what I should wear and how my hair should be done. I was more worried about practising my curtsy. Or should I bow?

I always loved clothes, and the day we left for Yorkshire, on the way to the station, I saw in a shop window a dear little black velvet cape from which peeped a lining of peach-coloured silk. I drew my mother's attention to it and begged her to give it to me. My dear mother made so many sacrifices for me, and when we boarded the train, the peach-silk-lined black velvet cape was mine. As for my hair, it was to remain in two long plaits over my shoulders. I was still only twelve, a few days from my thirteenth birthday.

Harrogate was a fashionable resort in Yorkshire where, in the classical Royal Pump Room, ladies and gentlemen gathered to take the curative sulphurous waters. Before the rehearsal I was photographed in front of the concert hall wearing my tailored coat and schoolgirl shoes, music-case in hand, hat on my head. Above and behind me, over the entrance to the concert hall, was the astonishing sight of my name in capital letters: MOURA LYMPANY.

At the hotel I changed into a white dress with a tiered frilly skirt, and white shoes and socks, while my mother tied a large white satin bow to the side of my head. With the velvet cape over my shoulders, I was ready to go to the concert, my very first performance in public.

I asked Basil Cameron: 'Shall I curtsy or bow?'

He replied: 'Whichever you feel happiest with.'

Included in the programme were Beethoven's Overture 'Prometheus', a suite by Handel and Beethoven's 'Pastoral' Symphony, and a Mrs Betty Bannerman was to sing an aria, 'J'ai Perdu Mon Amour', from Gluck's *Orfeo*.

I was not at all nervous. When it was my turn I walked on to the platform to see row upon row of faces before me, sat down at the piano, and played the concerto.

TWO PLAITS AND A SYMPHONY ORCHESTRA was the headline in the next day's *Daily Express*. The reporter described me as a 'quaint little figure' sitting among the Harrogate Municipal Orchestra at the huge grand piano, creating 'a piquant contrast to the symphonic thunders of which she was the centre'. The headline in the *Yorkshire Post* for Friday, 9 August was: CHILD PIANIST'S FINISHED WORK. And below came these comments:

> When these gifted young people essay works of a more exacting nature, we are apt to forget the music in marvelling at their mere ability. . . . Miss Moura Lympany was well-advised in choosing Mendelssohn's elegant piano concerto in G Minor . . . her youthfulness was symbolised by the large bow in her curly hair, gave a finished and pleasing performance. . . . The music is peculiarly youthful, one might say almost girlish. . . .

> Miss Lympany's technique was fluent, neat and she chose her variations of colour and force with correct taste.

And then, wonder of wonders, a letter arrived announcing that I had won the scholarship to the Royal Academy of Music and was to start there in September.

# 3

# 'I Want to Be a *Great* Pianist!'

In the early eighteenth century Dr Charles Burney tried to found an institution where orphans would be taught music, an idea his masters rejected on the grounds that music was an unnecessary luxury. Where the professional failed, the amateur succeeded: John Fane, 11th Earl of Westmorland, studied music at Trinity College, Cambridge, furthering his interest while Ambassador in Vienna and Berlin. Among his many compositions were eight operas, seven cantatas, innumerable madrigals and a Grand Mass. He founded the Academy of Music in the 1820s, gaining it its Royal Charter in 1830. In the summer of 1912 it moved to its present magnificent house in the Marylebone Road. 'Though a school does not set out with the intention of breeding a horde of Beethovens, Rubinsteins, or Paganinis,' wrote Tobias Matthay, 'yet if its teaching is efficient it will sooner or later hatch out a genius or two.'

Several distinguished pianists had preceded me to the Royal Academy of Music: Myra Hess, Irene Scharrer, Harriet Cohen, Clifford Curzon. On all floors from behind closed doors filtered through the sounds of strings, keyboards, brass and wind instruments, and singers of all kinds, practising all and every day. It was intoxicating to be a student in this atmosphere dedicated to good music. I adored it from the moment I arrived at Baker Street Underground Station and walked down the road past Madame Tussaud's to the handsome building with its spacious hall leading to the wrought-iron staircase embellished with musical motifs.

Ernest Read, who founded the famous concerts for children, was in charge of us RAM students for aural training. This was quite a rigorous business. My English was still rather uncertain. I had grown up learning my music in French and thought in that language. I always wanted to reply to his questions: *la noire, la croche, dièse* and *bémol,* instead of translating them in my mind first, and replying: quaver, semi-quaver, sharp and flat.

Miss Howell taught us composition, which, curiously enough, was a most unpopular subject with the students at the RAM. When the annual Academy competition for composition, the Hine Gift, was announced, I enthusiastically determined to enter. It was for a ballad, a musical setting of a poem selected by the committee and there were two months in which to compose it. The composition I worked on so tirelessly to perfect, and note down with meticulous care, a task in which I took almost as great a pride as the music itself, was the only entry, which was discouraging for the tutor. I won the prize and have treasured my little composition ever since, though it has never been performed in public.

During my time at the RAM I gave concerts, always announced as a 'child prodigy'. Basil Cameron, after my début at Harrogate, engaged me to play in Hastings, which was quite a red-letter day for me since it was there that Cameron had caused me to change my surname to Lympany, and in Eastbourne. By this time I had memorized the Grieg Piano Concerto, which I had studied with Ambrose Coviello, learned other works, and broadcast for the BBC. I was working hard, performing and studying, and practising between one and two hours every day. Nor was my general education neglected, for I was still a boarder at the Convent School of Our Lady of Sion, attended lessons there, and was expected to pass the same examinations as the other girls, which I did.

I had already made my début as a soloist, which meant I was living on several different levels. On the concert circuit I was now something of a celebrity as a child prodigy, and an English one at that, a considerable attraction for concert promoters. At the Academy I played the role of an ordinary student.

One of the joys of life and work at the Academy was the opportunities it presented of forging friendships and associations. Many trios, quartets and quintets formed themselves to play chamber music together. With the violinists David Martin, Max Gilbert, Frederick Grinke and Florence Hooton, who knew I was a good sight-reader, I played various sonatas. But I had little time, as I was always having to learn new solo works and rushing off somewhere to perform them. I had my school work too.

At the age of fourteen I played one of my own compositions at a charity concert. It was late December, at Anvers (Antwerp). My composition was an Étude in B Major, and I also played Chopin, Rachmaninov, Bach and Brahms.

There were regular concerts in the French baronial Duke's Hall at the Academy, and an important annual concert at the Queen's Hall when some of us were chosen to be seen, heard and judged. The annual concert was always conducted by Sir Henry Wood. In early June 1932, at the age of fifteen, I played the Grieg Piano Concerto in A Minor under Sir Henry's baton. Such a kind and encouraging master! The goodness of this great man is unforgettable. What a wonderful and humbling experience it was for me, a teenage girl. I adored him; he was so very nice to me.

The Academy's *Journal* described my playing thus: 'Moura Johnstone, with her feathery touch and sure musical understanding, gave the first movement of Grieg's A Minor Concerto Op. 16 as surely as Grieg himself would have wished to have heard it.'

Among many new pieces I learned at this time was a long sonata by the sadly forgotten English composer Benjamin Dale. He had been a student, professor, conductor and principal at the Royal Academy of Music. It is a tragic fate for many gifted composers that their work has to be rediscovered and repeatedly played to an audience before they become conscious that it exists at all. So much marvellous music has been created and lies buried somewhere waiting to be disinterred and revived. And yet many pieces of music remain effortlessly in the repertoire and are played too often, so that the public wearies of them and the musicians find it almost impossible to create a fresh performance of them.

For a sonata Dale's was unusually long – fifty-three minutes – and it was not an easy work to learn. I had difficulty with one particular passage: the repeat of the first theme towards the end of the first movement which led to the end of the movement. I could not get it right and practised it endlessly by itself, instead of the entire movement. This was a serious mistake, but I was only fifteen. The one thing all concert pianists fear is a lapse of memory. 'Memory is a series of links, of chains. If you have studied a work well, then you know that once you start, every phrase is a link that will lead on to the very end.' So wrote Tobias Matthay, the great teacher who was on the committee of management of the RAM and one of its professors.

I practised this isolated passage in the Dale Sonata on the day before the concert when I should have been resting and conserving my energy for the performance. So when I stepped on to the platform, I started playing and went straight to the end of the first movement just as I had practised. The great thing when one has a lapse of memory is not to stop, but to find one's way to the next vantage-point or theme. Somehow I played myself back to the beginning of the work and continued through the rest of the sonata with no more trouble. And happily, since the work was a new one and unknown to the audience, no one was any the wiser and I was vigorously applauded. Perhaps fortunately for myself and my budding career, the composer himself was not present.

The BBC, knowing I would play anything, asked me if I knew Armstrong Gibbs's 'Peacock Pie' Suite, lovely music settings of delightful poems for children by Walter de la Mare. I bought it, learned it and played it. The work is hardly heard nowadays.

One day my mother, who was always searching for ways to advance me in my career, read in *The Tatler* about the beautiful, music-loving Mrs Raffaelle Van Neck,[1] who had come from New York to live in London and gave glittering parties at which the standard of music offered the guests was high. My mother thought it would be helpful for me to play for Mrs Van Neck, and wrote to her. Mrs Van Neck invited some friends to hear me.

I was fifteen then, short, and a little plump. I wore a black velvet dress and my hair still hanging down my back in two plaits. Among the guests was a Mrs Harcourt,[2] who had been a professional pianist, and her two daughters, Diana[3] and Grizelda.[4] I was not nervous and played as I usually did.

When I had finished at the piano Mrs Van Neck invited me to stay to dinner. This kind of formal social occasion was absolutely new to me. At one point, when the dessert was served, Mrs Van Neck's butler handed me a tall silver object I had never seen before and had no idea what to do with. I turned it upside-down in my hands and castor sugar from the sugar-sifter, for such it was, rained down all over the table and my black velvet dress. I was mortified, but Mrs Van Neck and Mrs Harcourt were perfectly sweet and understanding.

The years at the Royal Academy of Music passed so quickly. At the end of the third and final year I won the Challen Gold Medal for the best student of the year. I wore a long

---

[1]Later Duchess of Leinster.
[2]Later Lady Harcourt, wife of Admiral Sir Charles Harcourt.
[3]Now Lady Menuhin.
[4]Later Mrs Louis Kentner.

white dress and vermilion grosgrain sash at the presentation ceremony. I was sixteen and my mother decided I must go to Vienna for further study, where I could also learn German.

The problem, as always, was money. How to pay for this? The travel, the tuition, the living expenses. The only solution was that I must earn the money. My mother wrote to a convent school in Vienna, which agreed to take me as a resident for nine months. In return for my board and lodging I would be expected to speak English to the girls.

On arrival in Vienna I made inquiries and obtained introductions to the best piano teachers in Vienna: Emil Sauer and Paul Weingarten. Which of them should I approach? Sauer was by then quite old and so I telephoned Weingarten. He invited me to go and play for him. I did so and he agreed to teach me, and then I had to make a confession. I had no money to pay for the lessons. He replied: 'You will pay me when you earn money at your next concerts.' This I duly did.

Weingarten was far from young but he was devastatingly handsome, with a mane of beautiful white hair coursing back from his noble brow. He had also a great fascination of manner. All the women were madly in love with him. I was very shy. I admired and revered him as a tutor. He was the great man who was teaching me to play the piano better. With him I studied that most romantic of works, the Piano Concerto No. 2 by Rachmaninov. He was entirely paternal towards me and even reproved me, saying: 'Don't be so academic – let yourself go!'

What can be said about Vienna that has not been said already a thousand times better than I can hope to do, in a great many books? This magic city was so wonderful. I was young and my time in Vienna was a time of discovery and learning. It was so beautiful to look at and all the musical associations were precious to me. All a musician's idols had been there: here Beethoven had lived; there Mozart; and the Strauss family had immortalized the city and glorious woods where at weekends the Convent students and I used to roam.

At this time, 1932, Hitler was beginning to rearm Germany, but any forebodings of that evil were not apparent to me, a vivacious English girl of sixteen utterly immersed in her music studies and intent for the rest of the time in enjoying herself as any girl would. The girls at the Convent were all about the same age as myself, light-hearted and gay.

One weekend in the country outside Vienna we stopped at one of those open-air restaurants, the kind in which Richard Tauber sang in his film début when a visiting impresario discovered him and made him a star. There were many vibrant talents in and around Vienna, but not all were destined to be discovered and become famous.

There was a piano at this restaurant and the girls asked me to play. So I did. I was playing for joy. And through this chance performance I made two lifelong friends. One was a girl called Ninon Leiter, who took me to meet her parents. They were so kind and affectionate they became like a second family to me. Just as those families had been during my early years in Belgium. The other was a Mr Slavetinsky who was in Vienna with his family on holiday from London, where he was head furrier at Calman Links. This shop had the great distinction of holding the Royal Appointment. He made himself known to me at this little open-air restaurant outside Vienna, gave me his card, and begged me to get in touch when I was in London again. Would I play for his boss, who was very musical and would be delighted with my playing? he asked me. I agreed.

I stayed in Vienna nearly a year. When I returned to London, I met and played for J.G. Links[5] and his two sisters. At this time, J.G. Links was studying the piano himself with Elsa Karen, who had been a pupil of Cortot. He took a great interest in my career and generously offered to pay for me to have a few lessons with Elsa Karen, which I did.

---

[5]J.G. Links, the authority on Canaletto, art critic and author of many distinguished books.

My time in Vienna had been well spent, and it was now decided that I should enter one of the several prestigious piano competitions: the Liszt Piano Competition in Budapest. It was the summer of 1933 and I was not yet seventeen. My mother once again overcame the financial obstacles by obtaining another engagement for me as an au pair to a family with a teenage daughter anxious to learn English. So I travelled to Hungary, where between trying to teach English to my pupil, and practise the formidable compositions by Liszt, I was fully and exactingly occupied.

These competitions always attracted agents and impresarios on the look-out for outstanding talent which they could encourage and on which they could capitalize. Wilfrid Van Wyck was present at the Budapest piano competition and he admired my playing, but I was not yet ready for these 'big guns' of the musical world. The first prize went to Annie Fischer who is still today considered to be one of the best, some would say *the* best, woman pianist in the world.

I adored Budapest, a hypnotic medieval city built on hills, an *artist's* city through and through, and cosmopolitan. The most romantic of rivers, the Danube, divided the old Buda from the new Pest. I felt and absorbed the magic of the Magyar tradition everywhere. Its instrument was the violin, the yearning music I had been unable to learn to love to play. Minstrels strolled about the cobbled streets casually playing heart-rending gypsy melodies. We had picnics on Margarit Island in the middle of the Danube and I was taken to the famous tea dances and to the even more famous swimming-pools.

English girls were very popular in Hungary and I was courted by handsome young men, all wonderful dancers and swimmers. I spoke English, French and German, and they all tried to teach me Hungarian. I could dance all night – and frequently did. I had a really wonderful time until one man went too far in pursuit of me with unfortunate and embarrassing results. He was not one of the lively young beaux with whom I swam and danced and picnicked, but the father of one of my girl-friends. I was rather suspicious of his intentions. However, I saw no reason to refuse my friend's invitation to spend the weekend at her family's country house. It was on the Puszta. We were to be a large party and I believed I could take care of myself.

In the rambling old house I found to my surprise and dismay that the bedroom I was shown into was in a quite separate wing from the rest of the guests and I became worried, so when I went to bed I locked my door on the inside and slept happily and fearlessly all night. The next morning, however, I found I could not unlock the door. I fiddled with the key, turning it this way and that, pulling and tugging helplessly at the handle. It would not budge. Then I began to panic; claustrophobia set in. I screamed and screamed: 'Let me out! Let me out!' Till at last someone heard me, and came and released me. This apparently trivial incident left me with a real horror of being shut in, and I try never to lock myself in anywhere, even the loo.

On my return to England from Hungary I was seventeen. My mother now resolved that even Bexhill-on-Sea was too far from London for me to be if I were to forge a career on the concert platform. It was clear from all shades of opinion she consulted that, incredible as it seemed, I had a real musical future. It was even then a competitive field for a musician, and it is a hundred times more competitive now. In the thirties the record industry had barely begun, and most music was heard only at live performances.

My resourceful mother found a little house to rent at Wimbledon, and I got myself a job as an accompanist to a singing teacher, a Miss Baldock, whose studio was at 46 Oakley Street, Chelsea. It was a short ride on the Underground followed by a twenty-minute walk. I enjoyed the work very much. Luckily it was not a full-time job, only a few hours a day. I needed to earn more to pay my way, and so I managed to get myself another job, teaching a little boy French for five shillings an hour. I loved children, and the little boy and I got on splendidly together. I was earning about £1 a week, out of which I gave my mother ten shillings. I was so proud to be earning a little money by myself that I went into the National Provincial Bank in Wimbledon and asked to see the manager. He readily admitted me to his office and contemplated me from behind a large desk. 'What can I do for you, young lady?' he asked benignly, and smiled when I told him I wished to open a bank account, my first. 'How much do you wish to deposit?' he then inquired and was surprised to learn it was all of one pound. But open an account with him I did.

Occasionally letters would arrive with offers of concerts. When such a letter arrived at Wimbledon for me, I would let out a blood-curdling whoop of joy! It meant I was making a little progress; I would have something to work for. I *never* refused any engagement. If I did not know the work I was asked to play I never confessed my ignorance, but rushed out and bought the music. And learned it. That is how I gradually built up a reputation for versatility.

This life of an accompanist/teacher ended when Ambrose Coviello suggested I sit for the Elizabeth Stokes Scholarship, again at the Royal Academy of Music, which I won. This time, being older, I was the contemporary of most of the students, but I still saw relatively little of them, as I resumed studying with dear old Ambrose Coviello.

Rafaelle Van Neck and Mrs Charles Harcourt, for whom I had last played before going to Vienna and Budapest, got in touch with me again, and soon I became a sort of society pet, playing for their 'At Homes' for all sorts of fees, sometimes five guineas or for as little as half a guinea. Through these engagements I began to frequent a milieu far above my social station and met more and more important people.

Sir Austen Chamberlain, who had been Foreign Minister, and Lady Chamberlain, after I had played at one of their receptions, when they heard I would be going back to

Wimbledon by myself on the Underground, insisted that I stay overnight. The Duke of Alba, the Spanish Ambassador, invited me to a reception. I was delighted to accept. I went by myself to this dazzling assembly at the beautiful embassy in the corner of Belgrave Square. All around me were a host of strange people. There was a long table at one end heaped with food beautifully laid out, and rows of glasses filled with champagne. I was petrified and there alone seized one glass and downed it, put it down and walked out of the room, deciding to go straight home. But on my way out I was stopped by a charming man, Sir Ronald Clive, Marshal of the Diplomatic Corps. 'Why are you leaving so early, my dear?' he asked.

I told him the truth. I was alone, I knew nobody, and dared not speak to anyone. He smiled kindly and offered me his arm. 'Come with me,' he suggested. 'I will introduce you to everyone.'

So I took his proffered arm and he led me in and I was soon laughing and talking. Ever since I have always found myself to be *en rapport* with the *corps diplomatique*. Had I not become a pianist, I might well have chosen to be a secretary to either a politician or a diplomat.

After only two terms of my second scholarship at the RAM my mother arranged for me to have private lessons with Mathilde Verne. This was a most important professional step. She and her two sisters were among the best teachers of piano in London. All three women had been pupils of the legendary Clara Schumann, wife of the great composer. Mathilde Verne had attended one of the first recitals by Paderewski and had been teaching for over fifty years.

My mother, and others, urged me to earn the fairly easy money I could have done by playing the piano for the tea-room at Lyon's Corner House. 'But', I protested earnestly, 'I want to be a *great* pianist!'

There are many levels of artistic attainment. Somerset Maugham wrote a brilliant short story about a young man who committed suicide because he passionately wanted to be a great pianist and could not face the truth when he was told his was a mediocre talent. I just wanted to play the piano and I wanted to play it better. I was never conscious of possessing exceptional talent. I simply followed the road that opened up before me. Without my mother, I should never have reached the point I had reached, where at eighteen I began to study with this great teacher, one of whose pupils was the Duchess of York.[6] The connection with Clara Schumann was an important one. Clara Schumann and Teresa Carreño were the forerunners of the modern woman concert pianist.

When she first heard me play, Madame Verne concluded that my technique was inborn. 'If you do not keep up your technical practice,' she warned me, 'you cannot possibly be free to interpret. In a Beethoven sonata, for instance, you will find humour, poetry, passion. How can you show all *that* if the muscles are not first trained and in trim, to produce what you want? Train your fingers, your muscles and your mind, and then play what you feel.'

Madame Verne laughed a great deal most infectiously but she was a martinet, adamant that I should play one hour's exercises every day, and practise four hours a day, one hour at a time, with an interval of one hour. These were: 10–11 a.m., 12–1 p.m., 3.30–4.30 p.m., and 5–6 p.m. I got so used to this routine that I found it hard to practise differently. The hours might change slightly but it was always two hours in the morning and two hours in the afternoon. Six o'clock was the time to relax completely, the day's work done. Unless an urgent concert or recording loomed, I never played or practised after seven o'clock, preferring to go to bed early and get up early the next morning, fresh for further work.

Madame Verne said my hands were 'enchanting'. A pupil with small hands as mine were, needed a different method of teaching from a pupil with large ones. 'I try to make my

---

[6]Queen Elizabeth, the future queen consort of George VI.

pupils *feel* the music,' she said, 'so that they need to express its beauty, and to work with them I have to understand my pupils, their natures and their characters, so that the lesson grows out of our personal relationship.'

Madame Verne was very keen on a *beautiful tone*. A *beautiful sound* was part of the Schumann tradition. And she inculcated into me that Schumann did not like all those soul-searching *rubatos* some pianists poured into their Schumann interpretations. 'You must *act* with your hands,' she instructed. 'The movements of the hands must result from the feeling behind them.'

'Who said pianoforte playing was easy?' she said sighingly to me one day. 'The piano is the most difficult instrument in the world to play. There are so many things to think about.'

Once I sat down to play to her the Schumann Piano Concerto, and I had just played the first entry, allegro affetuoso, and settled down to the next phrase, the beautiful solo, at about half the pace, when to my shock and dismay she tore my hands off the keys. 'Why are you playing half-time?' she demanded.

'Because it is always played like that,' I replied mildly.

'Has Schumann marked another tempo there?' she asked.

'No,' I replied meekly.

'Well then,' she instructed sharply, 'play it as it is written – the same tempo as the entry.'

For the second movement she wanted it to move (as did Schumann) and not held back at a snail's pace, as was the practice of so many pianists, presumably to show the extent of their emotion. 'Can't you *feeel* it?' she shouted at me.

And the third movement she wanted played at the given metronome pace (not very fast), so that every note could be heard and mean something.

She liked to watch my hands. They 'literally seem to dance on the keys,' she observed. 'The actual physical conditions must be easy and natural,' she continued. 'I like the arm to lie in a natural position – no crooking of the elbow to make a triangular sort of effect.' Many students needed stretching exercises and I was one of them. These improved my technique out of all recognition.

'As each finger in the upward sequence presses down on a key,' Mathilde Verne explained, 'it remains down until it is required to play the corresponding note in the downward sequence. The transference from one note to the other must be done with the utmost legato, and the tone must be beautiful throughout, and the hand and arm held without any stiffening whatever.'

She was insistent too that exercises should never be practised mechanically but in a lovely tone for every note. 'This can only be produced', she said, 'by thinking and listening. Beauty should be the aim of it all, and this comes from the heart as well as the head.'

Mathilde Verne said one day: 'I want you to give a recital at the Wigmore Hall.' The Wigmore was a lovely warm auditorium with, for the audience, the added joy of an art-nouveau mosaic apse over the stage. But for me, the artist, this was a great test. I was to give a solo recital and the audience was formed, not of kind society ladies but serious critical *cognoscenti*, not to mention the critics themselves.

In those days a recital cost about £50 or £60 and the only way to cover the expenses was to sell a great many tickets. Mathilde Verne knew many wealthy and influential patrons of classical music, and she had no difficulty in selling enough tickets.

The recital was a success.

When around this time I was engaged by the great Lancastrian conductor Sir Thomas Beecham to play the Schumann Piano Concerto at Croydon, I was alarmed by the tales I heard on all sides about him. He had a fearsome reputation. He was said to be an ogre who adored women but hated women pianists, although he had married one: Betty Humby, who had preceded me at the Royal Academy of Music. So, before the rehearsal I approached him with some trepidation. He stood on the podium, baton in hand, a dapper little man in shirt-sleeves and braces, gym shoes on his feet.

'Sir Thomas,' I quavered, not daring to look him in the eye but fastening my gaze on his imperial beard, 'I fear I play the concerto a little differently from the usual way.'

He fixed me with piercing blue eyes and said nothing.

'I play the first movement more moderato, the second a little quicker than usual, and the third slower than usual.'

He continued looking at me in silence for a moment, his rubicund features unruffled. 'My dear young lady,' he suddenly said in a suave purr, 'It is *your* concerto and I will follow everything you do.'

He was as good as his word.

Tragically, and very sadly for me, because I had grown so attached to her, and her tuition had meant a great deal to me, Mathilde Verne suddenly died. It was such a shock, such a loss. At eighteen I felt absolutely lost. I could only try to remember all she had taught me, and what I did not consciously recall had been absorbed into my playing and would never be forgotten.

# 4

# Uncle Tobs and the Ysaÿe Competition

Who on earth should I go to for tuition? I wondered. My next London appearance was to be with the British Women's Symphony Orchestra at the Queen's Hall. They had never heard of me and I had had to pass an audition. They also expected me to sell £50 worth of tickets. I was to play two works completely unknown to me: the Piano Concerto by Delius, an early work of his, and the Symphony on a Mountain Song by Vincent d'Indy, a scholarly French composer, protégé and lifelong friend of César Franck, the Belgian composer.

Selling tickets for the concert was quite easy. They had engaged a completely unknown girl, so I did my best, my mother helped and friends did the rest. The £50 was soon made up. The problem was tuition. The situation became urgent: the British Women's Orchestra concert at the Queen's Hall was almost upon me, and my playing of the two important works by Delius and d'Indy would attract critical attention. Critics are so important to an artist. They perform a great service to music and the arts. Without them, who would know about us, the performers? When they give a bad review it is really because they care passionately about the music. Often they are bored by the umpteenth performance of Handel's *Messiah* given by the local amateur choral society and a few semi-professional, aspiring soloists, but these fledgling singers may and sometimes do go on to great things, and it is the provincial critic who has spotted their potential and singled them out for notice.

The music critic Clinton Gray-Fisk, who was a personal friend of mine, knew of my distress and dilemma, and I sought his advice. Here was a case where a critic had heard and seen me play, recognized my ability and set me on the right road. Clinton Gray-Fisk's counsel was something for which I shall always be grateful. He was adamant: I must go to Tobias Matthay.

There was much talk of the 'Matthay Method', and I did not like what I heard of it. Matthay had written nearly twenty books purporting to explain his 'Method'. My old teacher Ambrose Coviello tried to explain Matthay's explanations in *his* book: *What Matthay Meant*. Matthay had been a Royal Academy of Music student, a popular pianist and composer before becoming a professor at the Academy. Legend has it that a dispute had occurred and he had publicly walked out, crossed the Marylebone Road and, followed by loyal students, founded his own school in Wimpole Street. In his book *The Act of Touch* he attempted a full-scale scientific analysis of the physical aspects of piano-playing, categorizing the various vertical movements into touch-species and laying great stress on muscular relaxation and forearm rotation. He was now over eighty and living in semi-retirement at his beautiful house High Marley, with panoramic views of the downs, in Haslemere. People who went to him for tuition came away exaggerating everything he had told them to do and so I had come to believe that the Matthay Method meant throwing oneself about at the piano, one's arms and hands flying all over the place. He had taught many superb pianists: Myra Hess, whom he called his 'prophetess', twenty-five years older than myself, a deeply serious, profoundly religious pianist; and Irene Scharrer, Eileen Joyce and Harriet Cohen had also gone to Matthay for tuition. So had Clifford Curzon. I obtained his books and tried to read them but could not understand them at all. One published in 1908 featured line-drawings of hands and fingers and arms doing extraordinary things, and pictures of a little boy wearing a sailor-suit seated at the piano. This last, later a professor[1] at the Royal Academy of Music, declared that Matthay's books had nearly put him off music for life. I did not want to go to Matthay. I felt sure he would want to change my way of playing and I had visions of starting from scratch again. However, I was becoming so nervous about the forthcoming concert I had to do something.

I fell in love with him the moment I saw him. He was so gentle, a darling little white-haired old man with a moustache, his eyes shining behind wire-rimmed spectacles, dressed exquisitely in a frogged black velvet jacket, velvet skull-cap and patent-leather slippers. He smiled sweetly at me, and patiently. His first lesson was a revelation. Seated beside me at the piano he explained more to me in one sentence than I had managed to discover from all his books.

'Uncle Tobs', as we all called him, insisted that all music must be memorized. Musical memory is a complex phenomenon. Copy on the piano, distrust of memory, makes it impossible for the artist to concentrate his whole mind on the search for the spirit of the music. Clara Schumann, whose own memory was unsure, used to sit on the sheet music as a safeguard when she played. Of the three main forms of memory used in playing – musical, visual and muscular – I had muscular and musical memory but not visual memory. My fingers often seemed to remember of their own accord what notes to play, and of course I sang the music in my head, as I have always done.

'Keep your mind on . . . the meticulously adequate sounding of the note or set of notes *due* that moment,' taught Uncle Tobs, 'and the next will then automatically and surely

---

[1]Professor Vivian Langrish.

loom up in your mind. If self-doubt sets in and a pianist commits the fatal blunder of trying to recall the next note, the sequential action is disconnected and breakdown inevitable.'

I must not think of anything else but the phrase I am playing. If I think of the next note, I break the chain of the phrase. If I think 'Isn't this beautiful!' while I am playing, I have lost the chain.

The concert with the British Women's Symphony Orchestra was a great success for me. I continued to study with Uncle Tobs for the next ten years.

Uncle Tobs showed me how to express my feelings, how to project what I felt. He taught me how to phrase, how to breathe, how to make 'hairpins' – that is, make a longer note sound louder than the next short note so that two notes never sound alike. He taught me how to put my finger on to the key before pressing it down so that the sound would be beautiful. He taught me to relax. The only thing he did not teach me was technique because, he said, I did not need to be taught technique. I had it.

He taught me to practise away from the piano. Silent practice he called it, without playing a note but with every note inflection and the actual playing processes vividly imagined. He liked to quote Robert Louis Stevenson:

Mark the note that rises,
Mark the notes that fall,
Mark the time when broken,
And the swing of it all;

So when night is come
And you are gone to bed,
All the songs you love to sing
Will echo in your head.

I had always marked my music and so I got into the habit of taking my music to bed with me and studying it silently as Uncle Tobs taught me. Overnight I digested it and the next day I really knew it.

One day I couldn't play thirds quickly enough.

'You're putting too much pressure on them,' he said. 'Try playing more lightly, as if you are a butterfly touching the keys, nearly staccato.'

He was quite right. They went much better.

Another day I was very downcast. I could not play octaves.

'You are thinking of them as octaves,' he told me. 'Play them very near the key, nearly legato, and don't think of them as octaves. Just imagine you are playing an ordinary tune.'

The octaves went much better and without mistakes.

His psychological approach was masterly and so subtle. He made me feel I could do anything. I even complained to him that he never seemed to criticize me.

'Every time I tell you something, it is actually a criticism' was his benevolent reply.

Many of the great pianists of the day played handfuls of wrong notes. It was said of d'Albert, who was a giant, that he could give a second recital with the wrong notes he had played at the first. Matthay never minded the wrong notes. 'Make music even if you play a few wrong notes' was one of his favourite sayings.

At this time Uncle Tobs chose me to play at the Queen's Hall in a concert of his best pupils. I played the second Brahms book of Variations on a Theme of Paganini and bewailed to Uncle Tobs the fact that I had played so many wrong notes.

'But you don't know how many things you did right!' he told me. He preferred to hear a few wrong notes if the performance had a bit of life.

Then I was to play the Fourth Piano Concerto by Beethoven. The opening phrase of this work terrifies every performer. One starts with a piano dolce chord, and the mood and nuances are sublime. Having tried for half an hour to get the mood I wanted into that phrase, I gave up.

Uncle Tobs did not believe in eight hours' practice a day and would say: 'If you can't do it in four hours, you will never do it.' He meant the brain could stand only four hours' practice per day. After all, one practised not only to get the notes right but to put the correct expression into the work.

What happens at a performance is that nerves start pouring adrenalin into the body and all emotions become more deeply felt. There is no doubt that practice makes perfect, but it depends on what kind of practice. Uncle Tobs said it was no good whatsoever practising when you were tired. Since one's brain imbibes everything put into it, there is no point in putting slipshod bad playing into it. It was far better to get up early and fresh the next morning and go straight to work.

One day I finished playing a piece for him with one arm way up in the air. Uncle Tobs gently took my hand and replaced it on the piano. 'Why don't you stay on the keys?' he said, with his charming smile. 'Lovely keys – stay on them.'

Then on another occasion I was rolling round at the piano, trying to bring out as much emotion as I could, when he put his arm round my shoulders. I gazed at him in surprise. 'The emotion has to come out,' he said gently, 'through your hands, not through throwing your body around.'

Every year a prestigious young musicians' competition took place in Brussels, in memory of the great Belgian violinist and composer Eugène Ysaÿe. One year it was for pianists, the next for violinists. June 1938 was the date of the next piano competition and Uncle Tobs suggested to me that I enter it.

This competition was open to all pianists throughout the world under the age of thirty. There would be twelve prizes. The first of three sections would select the semifinalists, the second select the twelve finalists, and the third stage find the prize-winner. My birth certificate had to be posted to the competition administrator, to convince them I was really under thirty, so I entered the competition under the name on my birth certificate and my passport, Mary Gertrude Johnstone, rather than the name everybody knew, Moura Lympany.

When Uncle Tobs told me that pianists from the whole world would compete and that the Russian Igor Oistrakh had won the previous year's violin contest, I was convinced I would not stand a chance.

'On the contrary,' Uncle Tobs said gently and quietly, 'I think you will have a very good chance.'

In my bank account at Wimbledon I had only £5 and this I drew out for my expenses. Happily, my dear old friends at 44 Rue au Beurre welcomed me back as their guest. There was our bond of affection and I could practise as much as I liked on their piano – the same piano I had used when I was six years old. In this regard pianists have a constant problem. Violinists, wind-players, brass instrumentalists, carry their instruments everywhere they go and so can practise anywhere. Pianists are dependent on finding a piano and hoping it will be properly tuned.

That year at Brussels there were seventy-eight pianists from twenty-four different countries, all borrowing pianos and practising the exacting programme we had been given day after day. One of the youngest was Arturo Benedetti Michelangeli from Italy who was only seventeen.

The competition was terrifyingly public. Her Majesty Queen Elisabeth of Belgium was its patron, since she was a talented violinist herself who had founded the competition. Ysaÿe had been her tutor. He had called her 'ma fidèle et devouée élève'. A few years earlier Belgian postage stamps had been issued, on one of which Queen Elisabeth was portrayed with her violin, while another featured Ysaÿe with his famous Guarneri. The Queen was present at all the early stages of the competition. From the seventy-eight entrants, twenty-eight were chosen for the semifinals, and I was one of them. Then the twenty-eight were reduced to twelve: six girls and six men, and I was still in with a chance.

Now came a very strenuous interlude. We twelve young pianists were each allotted a room with a piano in the magnificent royal palace of Laeken for one whole week leading up to the finals. During this time we had to learn a specially composed piano concerto, itself a great secret, for before our arrival in Belgium a competition had taken place among Belgian composers for the honour of creating a work for the occasion. Jean Absil's concerto had won this competition. Added to the task of learning this concerto by heart, we also had to prepare a second piano concerto of our own choice, and a biggish solo work.

So for one week the Laeken Palace in the centre of Brussels was a scene of tension and rang with piano music played all day on twelve separate pianos.

King Leopold and his mother Queen Elisabeth, both recently, tragically widowed,[2] were deeply interested in our work. They called on us to see we were comfortable and had all we needed. The Queen came every evening to our rooms, her camera in hand, to photograph us practising.

Lots were drawn as to who would play when in the finals. I was to play on the third day of the three-day event, so, to ensure I should not have an unfair advantage over the others, I was not allowed to see the music for the 'mystery concerto' until two days after the other contestants. I was rather worried how I should learn it, although I usually memorized music quite easily.

We were all young, and ambitious I suppose, but we were good-natured too, and when we saw each other at meals every day, we laughed and joked like all young people do. In the evenings we took turns playing the piano yet again, not classical music for the concert hall but dance music. The palace walls rang with our merriment. I loved to dance, and as we were six men and six girls I was never

---

[2]King Albert of the Belgians was killed on a mountain in 1934; Queen Astrid was killed in a car crash in 1935.

without a partner. One of the contestants was Jacob Flier, a shy young Russian who danced with me a lot. I liked him very much but he was so inarticulate, putting all he could not say into his piano-playing. Another was Emil Gilels, who called me 'Mouratscka', which means 'little Moura'– a term of endearment, for I was now twenty-one.

Before I received the Absil Concerto I asked one of the others how he was going to tackle it.

'Four bars at a time, then eight, then twelve,' he said.

So when at last the music was before me I tried to do that, always willing to believe others knew better than I did. I was mistaken. I could not make any headway and was wasting valuable time: the others had already had the music for two whole days. So I began to do what I had always done: played the piece through and through until it began to make sense to me. I practised the technical difficulties, and started phrasing the piece as Matthay had taught me. I also took the music to bed at night, following another sage Matthay counsel: 'Then you will know exactly what you want to do when you come to it on the piano.' Relaxed, sitting up in bed in my room at the Laeken Palace, I read the score over and over again till it was ingrained in my brain. I could hear it in my head the way I wished it to sound, then slept on it.

By the second day I knew the concerto by heart. I was practising five hours a day, one hour more than Uncle Tobs advised, but this was a very special time and I did not practise as long as Michelangeli. He practised a dangerous eight hours or more a day, an excessive amount.

The day before he was to play in the finals he came to us in great distress, his hands spread out before him. They were rigid and he could not move one finger. There was great consternation at the palace and a doctor had to be summoned to treat him. Michelangeli's hands were disastrously muscle-bound from too much work. He was advised to rest completely for twenty-four hours, and another pianist agreed to take his place so he could have an extra day to rest his hands before playing in the finals.

Emil Gilels, another of the Russian finalists, played the orchestral part for me so that I could be sure I knew the whole concerto by heart, and I did.

One day when we had been closeted indoors at our pianos all morning, while the June sunshine lit up the park outside, Gilels and I took half an hour off after luncheon to walk round the spectacular crystal house that enclosed the royal collection of tropical plants. The air was delightfully refreshing and, as we rounded a corner, on the path coming towards us was King Leopold, also out for stroll. 'I thought last night I heard strains that were not very classical!' he teased. It was true. We had been dancing foxtrots and waltzes and tangos till quite late, to Emil Gilels's scintillating piano-playing.

One of the two Russians was expected to win the competition. The rooms we occupied were not sound-proof and we could hear Gilels, who had a formidable technique, playing the Tchaikovsky Piano Concerto as only a Russian virtuoso could. Jacob Flier was playing the Rachmaninov Third Piano Concerto with the greatest sensitivity and passion. My chosen concerto was the Liszt in E Flat, and my solo work was Mendelssohn's *Variations Sérieuses*, chosen perhaps because Mendelssohn had been lucky for me and I had played him as a child in Belgium and at my début in Harrogate. Several of the pianists declared it was a poor choice. Nothing in it to show me off, they explained; no fireworks, no pyrotechnics. However, I could do nothing about that now.

Of the adjudicators the most important to me was Artur Rubinstein. He had known Ysaÿe well. They had had a kind of father-son relationship and had often played together, especially in London during the First World War. Rubinstein had known and admired Teresa Carreño, whose hands were strangely almost the same shape as his own. Rubinstein had rejected also the 'thin, solitary tone of the violin, dependent on an accompanist', as I had, for 'the divine instrument, the piano, with its polyphony and its harmony'. I idolized

Rubinstein. His playing was luminous, unearthly, yet fiery. He was so poised, so aristocratic, to me a divine being.

These competitions were not designed to find the best technicians but to select the most musical, the best all-round pianist. The test of committing to memory the Absil Concerto was a big hurdle. 'Memory is a series of links,' Uncle Tobs used to say, 'of chains. If you have studied that work well, then you know that once you start, every phrase is a link that will lead on to the very end.'

Of the twelve, only two played from memory. Sad to say, one of the final contestants, who had elected to play from memory, suffered a memory lapse during the Absil Concerto.

My mother and brother Tony came to Brussels for the finals. They were very proud of me and excited at my success.

When it came to my turn, first I played the Absil right through from memory without a fault. This was completely unexpected from a young Englishwoman; someone who had learned the piece by heart and played it within a week. After that I played the Mendelssohn, and perhaps because it did not 'show me off' but displayed my musical and interpretative qualities, it counted for me and it was an excellent contrast with the brilliance of Liszt in which I had every chance to show my technique.

At last we had each played and now we stood in a row on the stage to await the jury's verdict. We all expected the first prize to go to one of the two Russians, and it went to Emil Gilels. So we naturally assumed the second prize would go to his young compatriot, Jacob Flier. Then the announcement came: 'Mary Johnstone!'

I opened my mouth, rooted to the spot, speechless. I wondered for a moment who Mary Johnstone was, for I never thought of myself by that name. I glanced at Jacob Flier who was drawn, shaking and white as a sheet, and wished I could relinquish the prize and give it to him. The prize after all was not of such vital importance to me, but to him in Russia it meant everything. The third prize was his. The English pianist Lance Dossor came fourth.

The prize of a cheque for £350 I received from the hands of Queen Elisabeth, who graciously invited me to luncheon with her the next day. I could not help remembering that I had been chosen to play for her once before, at the Convent at Tongres during the festivities for the 700th anniversary of the Black Virgin. Denied that honour then, at the age of nine, here I was, twelve years later, having luncheon *à deux* with Her Majesty at the Laeken Palace.

I was forewarned that the Queen, who had been Princess Elisabeth of Bavaria, was a great stickler for protocol, which alarmed me not a little. She was now sixty-two. Then I heard that with musicians she was not so rigidly formal, for she felt that she was one of them, and they were all her friends or colleagues.

The piano competition provided much good copy for the press, and when the news that an unknown English girl called Mary Johnstone had won the second prize, the newspapers really made a big story out of it. Who was 'Mary Johnstone'? The music journalists had never heard of her and could find out nothing.

When I arrived at the Queen's private apartments in the palace, Queen Elisabeth, tall and slender, welcomed me with champagne and was as simple and charming as could be. I told her none of my friends would know I had won second prize, since everyone knew me as Moura Lympany. The Queen immediately gave orders that the journalists should be informed, and so the press had an even bigger story, for, by the name Moura Lympany, people in London musical circles knew me or about me.

We sat down to a most memorable meal – I even remember the menu. We began with poached eggs in a cheese sauce, followed by roast chicken accompanied by potato mousseline. Never have I tasted a purée so delicious; it must have contained masses of butter and cream. The champagne, my success, the relaxation of tension must have gone to my head. And to be fair to myself, nobody had instructed me in the correct protocol. I had no idea that I should watch the Queen and, when she stopped eating, that I should also stop. All I knew was that I was hungry and the food delicious. 'It's so good,' I heard myself saying enthusiastically to Her Majesty. 'May I have some more?'

'You do love your stomach, don't you?' remarked the Queen, rising from her chair, going to the sideboard and serving me herself.

Then I told her about the episode at the Convent. She remembered that she had expected a little English girl to play for her and was astonished to learn that I was the one.

The result of the competition had given my career a great boost. The British Council immediately wrote to me, offering me a series of concerts, but on condition that I played as Moura Johnstone. I flatly refused. I was known as Moura Lympany and I had no wish to start another career under a different name. Artur Rubinstein recommended me to his agent in Paris, so I received offers of engagements in Belgium, France, Italy, Holland and Scandinavia, Spain and Portugal.

Rubinstein opened all the doors for me. The most important was the entrée to the magnificent salon presided over by the Princesse Edmond de Polignac at her mansion, an 'Hôtel Particulier', in the Avenue Henri Martin. She had been Winnaretta Singer, the sewing-machine heiress, with such an early passion for music that for her fifteenth birthday she had begged for a string quartet. Her Sunday evening soirées were formal affairs attended by everyone of note in the worlds of music and theatre, ballet, opera and art. She was tall, haughty, formidable, but I loved her; she was serious about music and not a dilettante. With her was the equally grave, legendary Nadia Boulanger, the teacher to whom all the American composers went – 'The mother of us all,' they called her. The third of this legendary triumvirate was Comtesse Marie-Blanche de Polignac, the daughter of the *couturière* Jeanne Lanvin, lovely, fresh, also deeply serious about music, with a voice like an angelic lark. 'Hello!' said a frail young pianist. 'I'm Dinu Lipatti.' Everyone was charming to me.

Present at the competition in 1938 had been the Italian composer Prince Caetani and his wife Princess Caetani. When, later on, I was asked to play in Rome, I went to a cheap hotel and needed somewhere to practise. Prince Caetani di Bassiano was a member of the concert committee and offered me the use of his concert grand Steinway at the Palazzo Caetani. The Caetanis were most charming and kind to me and I had a very happy time in Rome.[3] I was on the crest of a wave following the Ysaÿe Competition[4] and utterly oblivious to the terrible events which were brewing in Europe.

I was travelling all the time, gaining fleeting impressions of many different people and places. Everyone was helpful and hospitable; places were briefly visited. Usually I saw only the railway station, the hotel, the concert hall; then the hotel, the railway station. There was no leisure and so much to think about apart from the music, which always came first. I had to look presentable – my hair, my make-up, my clothes. My hair was still long and I wore it in a heavy chignon on the nape of my neck. Audiences and critics liked a girl pianist to look pure and virginal, and I wore very simple dresses. I did not wear jewellery: the iridescence of long, dangling earrings in motion, for instance, would be a distraction in serious music-making.

Those finalists in the Brussels Ysaÿe Competition were to have remarkable futures. Gilels had a fabulous career. Jacob Flier returned to the USSR and, after he suffered an accident to one of his fingers, his performing career came to an end and he devoted himself to teaching. The only other English pianist apart from myself, Lance Dossor,

---

[3]Princess Caetani di Bassiano, an American by birth, edited the arts magazine *Botteghe Oscure*, so called after the name of the street where the palace was situated.

[4]Now known as the Queen Elisabeth Competition.

went to Australia, where he established himself as a soloist and teacher at Adelaide University. Yet it is very strange how many greatly gifted artists can start a career in a blaze of glory and then inexplicably fade away. A tragic case was that of a young Englishman, a most promising pianist who had won a prestigious competition but could not take the strain of a professional career and so, it is said, he put an end to his own life. As for the seventeen-year-old Michelangeli, who came seventh, he has matured into a dazzling virtuoso.

# 5

# War: The Colonel's Lady

'To gain for British artists the same prestige abroad as the best foreign artists enjoy in Britain.' This, I was told, was my mission when I went to Rome in 1939. I played Rachmaninov's Second Piano Concerto to great praise from the Rome press.

It soon became obvious to me that war was inevitable. My brother Tony was working in Antwerp in 1939 when the Germans invaded Belgium and he managed to escape from Antwerp and across to Ostend to board one of the last boats to England. He was nineteen and at once joined the Royal Air Force, becoming a fighter pilot. He adored flying, the excitement, the danger, the camaraderie of the other pilots. On one of his leaves he married an Austrian girl, an artist named Dita.

Joseph was only seventeen when war broke out. He joined up as soon as possible in the 'Buffs' and eventually was attached to the 4th Division of the Indian Army, 1st Lieutenant in the Royal Garhwal Rifles, known as the 'Garhwallies'. Three weeks before war was declared I travelled to play at La Scala in Milan, my first performance there and a thrilling début for me, despite warnings by friends that it was dangerous for me to go. They were unable to dissuade me and I was very well received. But a tour of Germany arranged for November was cancelled.

My mother had been living in Yelverton, Devon. A little-known wartime activity undertaken by Britons with a knowledge of languages was censoring overseas correspondence. This exacting occupation involved not only expert understanding of several languages but the ability to decipher often illegible handwriting. And to judge what information concerning the war contained in the correspondence should be deleted. 'Careless talk costs lives' was an official slogan of the time. Censorship offices were established at Liverpool, where my mother went to stay while engaged in this work. Her seven languages and knowledge of European countries were most useful.

All concerts were cancelled on the outbreak of war and at first I had no work. I wondered what on earth to do. From being one of the busiest concert pianists, constantly in demand, and travelling all over Europe, I was, as it were, grounded. The musical life of the country had come to a standstill: choirs, music societies and orchestras were disbanded. When the women's services were formed I contemplated joining the ATS, the WAAF, or the WRNS, but it was soon decided that the morale of the people at home desperately needed boosting, and with music.

The Germans had described England as 'the land without music', but the Nazis had driven music out of their country. Schoenberg, Bruno Walter, Klemperer and Schnabel had to leave, and hundreds of composers, conductors and instrumentalists had left too. Handel's oratorios were Aryanized and the statue of Mendelssohn in Leipzig removed.

Monsieur Edmond Jaminé – my 'Bonpapa' – had a grandson who escaped from Belgium through Spain. When he reached the frontier, he was put under severe interrogation from the authorities. He decided to pretend to be a French-Canadian to explain away his accent, and when his name was demanded of him, he spoke the only English surname he knew and that was mine: Johnstone. But he came to grief when asked to spell it, and was held for a while. Later he was released and allowed to come to England, where he joined the Royal Air Force.

'Music seems to be the one universal food that can take the place of all others at certain times,' wrote Yehudi Menuhin. 'In music the hearer lives another existence, apart from the doubts and worries of ordinary life. . . . People must need to be in need of music before they can really appreciate it.'

And they did need music now. Myra Hess, 'the great lady of the piano', had a brilliant idea. The National Gallery had been stripped of its treasures, which had been stored in some secret safe place in the country, and was now completely vacant and available. She went to see Kenneth Clark,[1] director of the National Gallery, and suggested to him that a concert once a week in the middle of London would be a great morale-booster to Londoners. He was most enthusiastic and thought the concerts should be not weekly but daily. So they set about organizing concerts for crowds of workers and troops. The admission was one shilling. By the summer of 1942 they had become an institution, and although the official limit on numbers was two hundred, audiences were so clamorous that they often numbered over two thousand. The Liverpool Philharmonic Orchestra were giving five times as many concerts as they had done before the war. The success of classical music in wartime England was unforeseen.

Every Sunday there was a concert at the Cambridge Theatre, arranged by Sidney Beer, a rich man with a passion for music and an unrealized ambition to be a conductor. Instead of spending his fortune on racehorses or a yacht, he spent it on creating an orchestra: the National Symphony Orchestra. It was a very brave venture because he was really an amateur in the true sense of the word.

Beer engaged me for two of the Cambridge Theatre symphony concerts, to play the Third Piano Concerto by

---

[1]Later Lord Clark.

Rachmaninov, a formidable work with more notes in it than any other piano concerto. The other work he wanted me to play was the Brahms Concerto in B Flat. Both works are technically the most difficult in the piano repertoire. I knew it would take me all of nine months to learn the Rachmaninov and six months to learn the Brahms. But I could not refuse such opportunities to master and play these great compositions and Mr Beer was happy to allow me the time to do so. They have since become among my most beloved and successful works.

I was constantly being asked to play works I did not know and which I had to learn at speed. This left me little time or inclination to learn works for which I did *not* have an engagement. I was renting a room at Paddington at this time, furnished with a few necessities and an upright piano on which I did all my practice.

The critics wrote that I played the Brahms like a man. They meant I had the strength of a man.

My policy was never to refuse an engagement even if I did not know the work. I relied on my ability to go out and buy the sheet music and learn it quickly. Edward Clark, of the Society for Cultural Relations with the USSR, unexpectedly got in touch with me early in 1940 with an unusual and exciting request. Would I play an unknown concerto by a Russian composer in a concert of Russian music? The conductor was to be the composer Alan Bush, whose own music was extremely popular in Russia. Bush was in demand and Russian music was to be popularized. Relations with the USSR were now vital to the progress of the war.

The concerto in question had first been offered to Clifford Curzon. Curzon at the age of seventeen had been a professor at the Royal Academy of Music, before going to Berlin to study with Schnabel. He was one of the few male pianists Uncle Tobs had taught. Curzon, now aged forty-seven, and a successful virtuoso, had so much work he refused the Khachaturian suggesting that I be approached. 'Moura Lympany learns so quickly,' Curzon assured Mr Clark. So I agreed, asking that the work, which was still in manuscript, be given to me as soon as possible, for there was only one month in which to learn it. Clark asked me where he should bring it and I told him I was going to the hairdressers, and would he bring it to me there? He said he would do his best and, as for a fee, I waved him away and said I would leave it to him and his committee to decide. To play the work was terribly important to me in my career.

I was sitting under the hair-drier at the hairdressers when into the salon burst Mr Clark, carrying a large parcel. It was the manuscript of the Soviet-Armenian composer Khachaturian's Piano Concerto. 'You look Russian!' he exclaimed at my reflection in the salon mirror. I began to study it then and there while my hair was in curlers.

I thought the Society for Cultural Relations with the USSR would probably offer me five guineas for this performance, so I was most surprised and grateful to be offered fifteen guineas, three times what I had expected. I learned this concerto for fifteen guineas but it repaid me a thousandfold.

The first performance, conducted by the composer Alan Bush, took place at the Queen's Hall in the spring of 1940. Miaskovsky's Sixteenth Symphony and Shostakovich's Fourth formed the remainder of the programme, but the Khachaturian Concerto created a sensation, eclipsing the other works. Nothing like it had been heard before. It was new, it was modern, it had fantastic pace, it was a thrilling work, and somehow it suited the warlike mood of the nation and the time, challenging and riveting. Uncle Tobs could not come to the Queen's Hall for the performance; now aged eighty-three he was too old and infirm. But the performance was broadcast and he sent me a telegram the next day which read simply: BEST CONCERTO SINCE LISZT.

The critics were surprised by my performance: 'Moura Lympany's virtuosity was as unexpected, as dazzling, and as agreeable to concertgoers in wartime London, as a friendly firework in the black-out.'

I had thus added a most valuable and innovative work to

my repertoire, which endorsed my reputation as a Russian interpreter. I was asked to play it everywhere I went and to record it for Decca.

The Soviet Ambassador, Mr Ivan Maisky, a stocky, smiling man, was ecstatic, not only because of the artistic success of the concerto but because of the excellent cultural links which its popularity helped to forge. Maisky deluged me with enormous bouquets and almost equally large boxes of caviare, a luxury delicacy in wartime. I received invitations to innumerable Embassy receptions. With my Russian Christian name and my mother's and aunts' background of having lived in Russia, it was assumed that I was Russian, and that I specialized as a Russian interpreter.

Later that same year Ambassador Maisky was an honoured guest at the Savage Club, which did not admit women. Mark Hambourg played the piano and Parry Jones sang for him. 'In my country,' Maisky told the assembled guests, 'artists have a vital place in the war effort.'

The Rachmaninov and Khachaturian concerti really established me. The public and the media alike need to put artists into a pigeon-hole – 'She's a Bach specialist', 'He's an Arthur Bliss interpreter', and so forth. I had played concerti by English composers but I never played the Arthur Bliss Concerto because Solomon was the leading exponent of that work. He was always asked to play it, and nobody else.

I had become a Russian specialist, recording all the Rachmaninov Preludes, which not even the composer had done. That added to my reputation. Quite soon I was being asked to play the Prokofiev concerti, the First and the Third, and having mastered these, I added the Fourth – which is for the left hand – to my repertoire too. Then I was engaged to play a relatively simple work, the Second Piano Concerto by Shostakovich.

The conductor Erich Kleiber was a Beethoven specialist. 'How', I once asked him reverently, 'did you discover you had an affinity with Beethoven?'

Kleiber laughed. 'At the age of nineteen,' he replied, 'I was conducting the Berlin Orchestra, and I used to give them Beethoven. The critics wrote that I was not mature enough to conduct Beethoven, but I took no notice and went on giving them Beethoven every Sunday, with the result that I am now acclaimed as a Beethoven specialist!'

Meanwhile I played all over England, to the factory-workers in Yorkshire, dock-workers in Hull, and everywhere I was sent.

This was a very strenuous time, and a most exhausting way of life, when there was little comfort and convenience for an artist travelling and working alone. Petrol rationing meant that there were no taxis. I had not yet learned to drive so had no car and probably would not have been able to get the petrol to run one anyway. Trains were unheated and there were not many of them. Buses likewise. One of the greatest problems was food rationing. I needed energy with which to play the piano like everyone else did for their war-work, but I had no home life at 10 Orsett Terrace, Paddington, and was dependent on what I could buy whilst travelling. Often, like everyone else, I did not have enough to eat, and so became debilitated, and my already highly strung temperament caused me to become even more nervous. The migraines I had suffered from when I was younger, recurred with a vengeance. The best treatment was to lie in a darkened room for several hours. I had little chance to do this; there simply was no time and I just worked through them with a couple of aspirins. Concert halls and theatres were so cold and draughty I sometimes played wearing a fur coat with mittens on my hands.

Clothes too were rationed and, in order to maintain my concert appearances, I had several gowns made for me from furnishing materials, velvet and brocade, which one could purchase without clothes coupons. These were a great success.

Eileen Joyce and I were contemporaries. She was an intensely beautiful pianist, and in her case like mine it was the nuns at her convent school in Australia who had fostered her talent. Eileen also liked to dress in glamorous gowns, and indeed changed her gown during the interval of a concert. The press tried quite hard to make us into rivals and even to create a feud between us and were surprised when neither of us would play their game. We were colleagues in the cause of good music and respected each other's abilities. The great romantic piano concerti were the basis of our popularity and resulted in several successful feature films which popularized them even more: *Love Story* with Stewart Granger, and Margaret Lockwood as a concert pianist, in which she played the Cornish Rhapsody; *The Seventh Veil* with Ann Todd and James Mason; and, best of all, *Dangerous Moonlight*, in which Anton Walbrook played not only a famous Polish pianist but one who was also a heroic pilot. This last featured the Warsaw Concerto, played by Louis Kentner, which was to become the most famous piece of music to emerge from the war, composed by Richard Addinsell. Eileen Joyce, now married to a theatrical agent, had the good fortune to play Rachmaninov's Second Piano Concerto for *Brief Encounter* and *Seventh Veil*; while Harriet Cohen played the Cornish Rhapsody. Most serious pianists believed the popularity of Addinsell's Warsaw Concerto was beneath them artistically, but time has proved them wrong.

I had to go on; I had my living to earn. London during the time of the air raids was terrible. The nights were endless with bombs dropping everywhere and crowds wrapped in blankets sleeping in rows along the Underground stations. The night that never ended was 10 May 1940: I had slept under my piano all night. The next morning I was due to attend a rehearsal with orchestra at the Queen's Hall for César Franck's Symphonic Variations. I had never played this composition before, and it had already come to mean a great deal to me. I felt it was peculiarly mine in a way no other piece of music had been before. César Franck was a Belgian, born in Liège, where I had studied as a schoolgirl.

Off I went through the streets to find, when I reached Langham Place, that the Queen's Hall had received a direct hit the night before. A stick of bombs had destroyed the whole block, including Augner's music publishing house. All that met my gaze next to All Souls Church, which had miraculously survived, was a ruin from which rose a thin plume of smoke, for the fire was still smouldering. In dismay I stood there helplessly, to be joined by the members of the orchestra and others. The distinctively semicircular building that had been the Queen's Hall meant so much to all of us; we had all played there since our student days. Standing crookedly among the ruins was a music-stand bearing sheet music: 'Loveliest of Trees' by Muriel Herbert.

The concert, unrehearsed, took place at 2.30. The conductor, Maurice Miles, the orchestra and I were lent the Duke's Hall at the Royal Academy of Music instead, so off we went to the Marylebone Road. I had had no cause to go there since my student days and it seemed extraordinary how much had happened to me since. There were the boards hanging on the wall bearing all the names of former students and the years they had attended the Academy. My name was listed four times: Moura Johnstone (Ada Lewis Scholarship); Moura Johnstone (Elizabeth Stokes Scholarship); Moura Johnstone (Hine Gift for Composition); and Moura Johnstone (Challen Gold Medal); all in gilded letters.

About this time I sat for my portrait to the painter Geoffrey Watson. He planned a full-length study in oils. I wore a white dress for the sittings in his studio in Chelsea, my hair braided and coiled in a coronet round my head. The artist was a tall, thin man, dressed in sandals, open-neck shirt and crumpled corduroy trousers. The portrait was beautiful when it was finished and framed, and a friend took a photograph of the artist standing before it, paintbrush in hand, I in my grave pose, looking ethereal, sitting up on a dais, a strangely Pre-Raphaelite composition. To the artist's and my distress, a bomb fell in Chelsea and destroyed the portrait along with his studio. Later, Watson begged me to sit again for him. I was leaving for Australia in three days, but he was so insistent that I let him come to do a simple portrait sketch in red chalk while I was practising my programmes. At his request I wore a concert dress.

The war ground inexorably on. In 1939 I had met a charming man, Lt-Colonel Colin Defries, who had survived the First World War in which he had flown in the Royal Flying Corps. He was a passionate amateur musician, a pianist, and attended all my concerts. He had been a great friend of Benno Moiseiwitsch, who for two years had been his parents' guest in their London house. Colin had cherished the ambition to be a professional pianist himself, but, when the First World War ended, he had studied for a degree in engineering and had successfully launched his own business, manufacturing small parts for aircraft and Rolls-Royce. We became great friends. He was an ardent, courtly admirer, and a wonderful host. After my concerts he would arrange a reception for me with military efficiency. At these times I would be on a 'high' after my hard work, and then I would relax and greet all my friends and fans. These were most important occasions. I could not do it by myself then and Colin enjoyed providing the background for me.

Colin could see that the strain of years of work added to the perils of war were telling on me and that I was nearly at the end of my tether. He told me I was terribly in need of someone to look after me. He proposed to me and so I faced a difficult decision. I was not in love with him and told him so, but this did not deter him. He was sixty years old, a tall man with a small military moustache. He seemed to me to be a heaven-sent bulwark against the difficulties of my life. He was patient while time passed and I considered his proposal. He was so kind and helpful and I grew to love him. He understood me perfectly, and my music too.

'Suppose I fall in love with a younger man?' I asked him.

He winced as if I had struck him by reminding him that he was thirty-two years older than I was. He replied gallantly that of course he would release me. 'You need a proper home,' he said, 'so you can give all your energies to your music instead of worrying about earning a living.'

I knew this was true and so I at last agreed to marry Colin.

It was the usual sort of wartime wedding: a registry office ceremony, no bridal gown, for clothes coupons were required to buy every yard of material, no bridesmaids, only a few friends present, and no honeymoon.

The one word Colin had spoken to me which had embedded itself in my consciousness was 'home'. I hardly knew what that word meant. It sounded beautiful to me and I clung to it while we set about finding somewhere to live. We house-hunted within commuting distance of London and found a delightful house at Oxshott in Surrey near his business. The address was Whiteacre, Knott Park.

Colin was a generous man but not at all rich. He had his Army pension and salary as managing director of his firm. The house at Oxshott was for sale at £4,000. It had a garden and I had set my heart on it. Colin paid a deposit of £1,000 but, because of his age, he could not borrow the rest. So I took out a life insurance policy and borrowed the balance of £3,000, and the house was ours. The title-deed was in my name, as I had provided three-quarters of the purchase price.

For the first time in my life I had my own home. A real home. It was wonderful. I was very happy in a kind of father-daughter relationship. Colin had an excellent business brain and took care of all the paperwork concerning my concert engagements and the financial and accounting details, a quite heavy burden I was only too grateful to delegate. It was a great relief to me. And we partnered each other at the piano, having installed two pianos in the drawing-room. Colin was at his office all day and when he came home at 4.30 we would have a cup of tea together, talk over the day's events and then practise from 5 to 6 p.m. He would play the orchestral accompaniments to my concertos, which was a great help to me. His advice was always good too. Like Uncle Tobs's it was benevolent, avuncular, and he came with me to all my concerts and made careful notes while I rehearsed, reading them to me afterwards.

'You should play louder in the andante.'

'You should play softer in the adagio.'

'You should play clearer in the repeat of the theme.'

'You should play more expressively, more passionately in the cadenza.'

It was said that Colin pushed me too much, but this was neither true nor fair. He enjoyed the role of consort to a star of the concert platform and was wonderfully supportive and protective.

Edgar Allan Poe in his essay *The Philosophy of Composition*, wrote:

> It is in the nature of a person of feeling to want to do everything by unbridled impulse, as it is in the nature of the intellectual to love to fill up a form. The real artist is a combination of the two. Cold intelligence and hot enthusiasm are two oddly-matched steeds for the chariot of Phoebus Apollo, but they must be taught to go in double harness, neither leading, but side by side and mutually helpful.

This is how Colin and I worked: our two pianos side by side, he playing the orchestral parts and I the solo.

Colin gave me the greatest help and a home, a base, where I could study quietly without worrying about the next bill to be paid. It was also said that musically I got on so well because my husband helped me so much. But my career was already established before I met Colin. It is true that I became emotionally and intellectually very dependent upon my husband. Colin Defries was a forceful character and an authoritarian figure accustomed to command and to be obeyed. My own father had been absent from most of my childhood and my mother had run everything. So Colin provided this significant role in my life and development.

At home I had never been so blissfully happy. I hated anything that took me away from that house at Oxshott. When I came back from being on tour exhausted, Colin would make me stay in bed for thirty-six hours. I learned to cook and be a housewife and I loved and tended my garden. On Sunday evenings Colin and I were 'At Home' to friends and colleagues, who came down from London, and I would play informally for them. Maurice Edelman, then a young political journalist on *Picture Post*, came to see us at this time, and wrote a feature about me:

> The word 'attack' is used to describe certain aspects of a musician's style. It is the quality which even the best woman performers lack. But in every human activity there appears at some time a gifted woman who shows herself the equal of men in the vigour of her technique. Lenglen as a tennis player and Earhart as a flier are two examples of women who have learnt and applied the mechanics of their art like men. In the same way Moura Lympany has an 'attack' which equals that of any male pianist.
>
> Watch her at a concert waiting to begin a cadenza at the end of an orchestral passage. She is poised, her hands raised, her eyes on the conductor: she is counting and yet she is absorbed in the wave of sound, remote from the tense audience, remote from the draughty wings, remote from everything but the music of which she is part. She waits, and then, with the exact timing of an athlete or a cat, she pounces on to the note. Her technique is as sparse, as appropriate, and as satisfying as the notes of a Bach fugue.

I remember playing at the Royal Albert Hall one afternoon – there were no evening concerts on account of the blackout – and afterwards changing into a pair of trousers and going straight out to do some gardening. Round the back of the house I had wired in a patch to make a chicken-run where six chickens scratched about, all rushing to the wire-netted door and clucking a greeting, while my dog Jock barked at my heels and my tabby cat purred and prowled round my ankles under the apple tree. I had four ducks, too, which roamed free in the copse at the end of the garden. I was a real home-bird.

We were allowed only one egg per month on our ration books and so the fresh eggs from our hens and ducks were most useful. Protein is the energy-giving food, and so, when I went into the provinces to play, I would take a couple of eggs with me and swallow them raw. Colin used to say that when I was nervous and ruffled, all I needed was feeding and then I would be all right.

I was so happy in my little world at Oxshott. The only thing missing that I longed for was a child. All my girl-friends knew I was longing to have a baby, and Colin knew this too. Colin, benevolent in everything else, was on this subject implacable. 'Any woman can have a baby,' he said sternly, 'but nobody can play the piano like you.' Colin made all the decisions in our life, so I gave up hope of ever having a child.

Colin was a very good gardener and I learned a lot from him. In his masterful way, he would direct operations. Everything was carefully planned. He also taught me punctuality, terribly important for an artist who must arrive at a strange town and then an unknown concert venue, all prepared to give of her best at the piano. As in everything else, he figured out a system for me thus: 'You work out first how long it will take you to get to your appointment, always allowing the maximum time, then you add the time it takes you to dress and you start accordingly.' After mastering this I never found it hard to be on time.

The novelist and historian Peter Vansittart met Colin at this time. Colin was a keen tennis and squash player and belonged to the Hampstead Squash Club where Vansittart was a member. If I was away for a couple of days playing in the provinces, Colin would go and play an evening's squash. Vansittart was then in his late twenties, and Colin talked about me to him, giving him the impression that I was 'meek and retiring'. I suppose I was. All I cared about was my music and my husband and our home.

Despite the war, ordinary social life at home still went on. Jumble sales, coffee mornings in aid of good causes, usually connected with the war effort, were plentiful in Surrey, and I tried never to refuse any request to play. When a Mrs Winn of Esher asked me to give a recital in aid of something, I forget what, I agreed, not realizing she was the mother of Godfrey Winn, the popular journalist, then a naval officer away at sea. Afterwards she told him: 'Miss Lympany not only played beautifully, but she seemed to enjoy herself so much. One felt at the time she was taking as much trouble for us as though it was a packed Albert Hall. To me that is always the test of the star performer.'

I recall recording the Mendelssohn Piano Concerto in G Minor under Kubelik, supervised for EMI by Walter Legge. The sun was shining outside, I remember. Legge had a vision, a wonderful vision, he was so sensitive. When I began to play I could see the expression on his face. I knew something was wrong. I played on and then he stopped me and confronted me. 'It's dreadful, Moura!' he exclaimed. 'You're playing like a schoolgirl!'

I was dismayed. The Mendelssohn Concerto was, of course, the one with which I had made my début at Harrogate when I was twelve years old. 'What shall I do?' I asked Walter.

'Go home,' he advised, 'and spend the whole weekend thinking about it. It's got to be full of fire.'

After we had recorded it to his satisfaction, he took me aside.

'Moura, I want you to record the Debussy Préludes.'

I would not listen. My confidence in myself was at such a low ebb. 'Oh but Walter,' I protested weakly, 'Gieseking has done them so beautifully. I simply couldn't play them as well as he does.'

'Moura,' Walter began again patiently, 'I want you to record the Chopin *Fantaisie*.'

Again I demurred. 'Oh, but Walter,' I wailed, 'Cortot has done it so beautifully. I simply couldn't play it as beautifully as he does.'

Years were to pass before I took his advice.

Then I was to record Litolff's famous scherzo for HMV, which Walter Legge was supervising. After I had played this quick, brilliant short work, giving it all I had, Legge said to me: 'Moura, could you play it again, a bit faster?'

'Faster!' I echoed, breathless and amazed. *'Faster?!'*

I tried, for Walter, to do just that, and he was satisfied. And that is the record which was passed.

My younger brother Joseph had been promoted to the rank of acting captain. Early in 1944 I had an engagement to play the John Ireland Piano Concerto at Bristol. It was rare for either of my brothers' leaves to coincide geographically or any other way with my concerts, so they had not often seen me play. On this occasion, however, Joseph had embarkation leave, which sounded rather ominous. He was determined by hook or by crook to get down to Bristol to see me, and hitch-hiked all the way.

Bristol was a city of importance in our family history. Our grandfather, Dr John Salcombe Johnstone, had retired there after selling the family estate at Sandhurst, Gloucester, but he had still continued to practise medicine. Although I never saw the house, I heard about it from my father. It was at Tyne Path, Redland Road, a corner-house with a passiflora climbing round the front door, and a mouth-tube for patients to announce their presence to the receptionist. Our aunts had gone to school at the local convent and two had become nuns: Sister Mary Bede of the Poor Child Jesus, a Dutch order founded at Simpelveld, at St Michael's Convent, North Finchley; and Sister Mary John, at the Convent of Our Lady, Southam, in Warwickshire. It was in Bristol that our grandparents had died and were buried.

Joseph knew he would at any moment be posted to Italy with his regiment. The John Ireland Concerto is a supremely English work. There is a beautiful melody at the beginning of the second movement, and when my darling brother came to see me after the concert there were tears in his eyes. 'You played as if you were crying,' he said, 'and I cried too.'

The remembrance of that concert in Bristol is inextricably linked with my last memory of my beloved brother.

Joseph was twenty-two, a beautiful young man, handsome, idealistic, deeply religious. Some of his fellow-officers were cynical and jeered at him because he always attended Mass on Sundays and loved to listen to my records instead of boozing in the mess. In Italy on one of his leaves he went to stay at the Palazzo Caetani with the Prince and Princess Caetani di Bassiano who had been my friends after my first concert in Rome. Their only son, a charming boy, had been drafted for military service in the Italian war against Ethiopia and been killed. They were still desolate from the dreadful blow and welcomed my brother as a son.

Once, when Joseph was on a reconnaissance on a remote Italian mountain with two of his fellow-officers, 'Cliff' and 'Sandy', the three young men were very depressed, being far from home with an uncertain future and outnumbered by enemy forces. Suddenly Joseph began to sing Gounod's 'Ave Maria' and, when he had finished, 'Cliff' followed it with 'Blue Champagne' and they cheered up.

At the Battle of Rimini the Allied forces suffered terrible losses, as did the Germans and Italians, and the British decided to ask for a temporary truce so they could bury their thousands of dead. Someone had to be found to walk across the no man's land stretch of ground between the armies, someone who would carry aloft the white flag that signalled a peaceful overture and also speak German to negotiate with the enemy. Joseph volunteered.

His men watched as he strode over the hill, holding the white flag aloft though limp in the sweltering Italian glare. It seemed a long way and every step he took he feared might be his last. His men thought he would be shot down at any moment. Eventually they saw him return, exhausted, drawn, but having completed his mission. A twenty-four-hour truce had been arranged and agreed. There was a much-needed respite for them all.

But after the truce the fighting began again. The thunder of the guns was relentless and, in an ambush, my brother Joseph was killed.

He had given my name and address as next-of-kin. In the autumn of 1944 a telegram arrived for me marked PRIORITY OHMS on the yellow envelope:

> DEEPLY REGRET TO INFORM YOU OF REPORT RECEIVED FROM CENTRAL MEDITERRANEAN AREA THAT CAPTN C J JOHNSTONE BUFFS ATTACHED INDIAN ARMY WAS KILLED IN ACTION ON 23rd OCT 1944 STOP THE ARMY COUNCIL DESIRE TO OFFER YOU THEIR SINCERE SYMPATHY STOP
>
> UNDER SECRETARY OF STATE FOR WAR

I was distraught and inconsolable but my husband Colin did his best to comfort me. Worse was to come, for we had to go to Devon to break the news to my mother. Joseph had been her favourite son, her little darling ewe lamb, and she was now aged sixty-four. How we got through that terrible time I shall never know. My mother never recovered from the shock of her son's death. Tony too had adored Joseph, in an unusual way for an elder brother. Joseph had that quality of character so rare; his men idolized him. He always cared for them and saw they were fed and comfortable before he was, as a good officer should. Tony, reckless, feckless, happy-go-lucky, survived the war unscathed, but he resolved that at some time in the future he would make a pilgrimage to our brother's grave at Rimini.

# 6

# Mrs Bennet Korn, New York

Paris was liberated in the spring of 1945 and five weeks later Colin and I were on our way to the French capital where, under the auspices of the British Council, I was to play the Rawsthorne Piano Concerto No. 1, a work I learned for the occasion, and again the Khachaturian, under the baton of Sir Adrian Boult with the Orchestre du Conservatoire.

The Germans had occupied every hotel in Paris and had not long left, so these were virtually uninhabitable. Where were we to stay? We were advised we would be quartered with a family. The brother occupied the first floor, his sister the second. Colin and I were guests of the brother and his wife, Alexis and Suzanne Rateau.

There was no fuel, there were no cars, no petrol and little food. Or drink. Gunfire could still be heard in the distance at night. The war was not yet over. But Paris was in a state of high excitement and, despite the privations, my hostess was determined to make the most of the occasion of my concert. Dressed in a stunning couture gown, festooned with long-hidden family jewels, Suzanne Rateau clambered behind her husband, wearing white tie and tails astride his motorcycle, and off they went to the salle, le Théâtre des Champs Élysées, where I was to play Rawsthorne's Piano Concerto No. 1. It was an important and impressive event. The French musicologists were very keen on Rawsthorne, comparing him favourably with Benjamin Britten. The history of the theatre enthralled me: here had taken place the incredible first performance of Stravinsky's ballet *Le Sacre du Printemps*, which had caused riots. Its beautiful allegorical frescos, its magical lights, the ranked tiers of seats imbued with musical legend, made it thrilling. Now I was adding another chapter to its history. I was English yet I had been chosen to play at this time in Paris when French patriotic feeling was at its height.

After the concert Colin and I attended a dinner-party in my honour at which I found myself seated next to a charming man. 'I have a couture house,' he told me. 'Would you like to come and see me and choose a model for your next concert?'

'How gorgeous!' I exclaimed.

'My name is Robert Ricci. Nina is my mother.'

To my husband across the dinner-table I called above the hubbub of conversation: 'Darling! Monsieur is Madame Nina Ricci!' Everyone laughed.

The next day we went to the salon, where I chose a beautiful dress: white organza encrusted with black guipure lace and embroidery, very *jeune fille*, and I vowed I would wear it when I made my début in the United States. The long years of the war had prevented this extension of my career, but it had not harmed me, for I had gained so much in experience from playing under all sorts of conditions and learning unusual works.

I adored the Ricci style and went back again and again to the salon, usually to choose a model in a sale, as they were far too expensive and I could never buy them then and there. Robert considerately arranged for me to pay for them in instalments. There was one of black velvet with shell paillettes embroidered all over the skirt. It was so lovely and when I first saw it I was horrified by the price. Robert refused to sell it to anyone else. 'It's yours!' he told me. I still have this dress and cannot part with it. It has been let down and out several times and even had pieces let in and I still love to wear it. Another Ricci gown I wore was made from yellow lace encrusted with sequins with a cape of lime-green satin. This, too, Robert absolutely declined to sell to anyone else.

I played at the Proms the year the war ended, the summer of 1945. The Czechs were planning the Prague International Festival, the first international music festival to take place after hostilities ceased, in 1946. I was asked for. I was thrilled to accept this singular honour and excited at the prospect of meeting the foreign musicians who were also going to appear: Charles Munch, Ginette Neveu, Nicole Henriot – these last two still in their twenties. I had already played with Munch at one of the concerts du Conservatoire in Paris.

The young Czech pianist Rudolf Firkusny was to be the chief soloist at the festival 'Prague Spring'. We met at an Anglo-Czech gathering in London hosted by Sir Cecil Parrot, the diplomat and Czech scholar. Firkusny had been the great friend and inspiration of the composer Martinu. Both had been in Paris in the twenties and thirties. Firkusny, sponsored by Dr Jan Masaryk, had grown to great prominence. Martinu had composed his Second Piano Concerto for Firkusny, premièred at Prague in 1935 before both composer and pianist were blacklisted by the Nazis. Firkusny had managed to escape to America where he had spent the war years in safe exile, and now a jubilant reunion was planned between Firkusny and Martinu.

The pianist arrived from America just twenty-four hours before the reception, exhausted, but had spent the entire day in the recording studios. Later that evening he was due to broadcast a solo recital for the BBC. He was greeted like a hero by his compatriots at the party, generously talking to everyone with the greatest ease. Pressed to play, he gave the guests an impromptu recital of Czech folk-music and I admired his playing enormously, especially his lovely soft tone and touch. In conversation I found him simple and natural.

The British Council, who were sponsoring the British contingent, asked me to play a British work in Prague. In addition to the John Ireland Piano Concerto I decided to play the Benjamin Dale Sonata. Both these works had been important in my life. Bach and Ravel were also included in my programme. Among my colleagues also going to Prague were Sir Adrian Boult and the Aeolian Quartet, and Leon Goossens, considered by many to be the greatest oboe player in the world, a charming, courtly companion.

On the morning of 20 May I left Colin at home at Whiteacre before 8 o'clock to go to London for the rendezvous at St James's Street, where we assembled to await the coach that was to take us to Croydon Airport. We were all in high spirits. The war was over and although there was still food and clothes rationing and utility furniture was all that could be bought, the festival we were about to help launch in Czechoslovakia seemed to herald a brighter future for the world in Europe. The sun was shining in London and we felt so gay. At Croydon we all trooped up the steps into the Transport Command aircraft, to be handed a packet of sandwiches each to eat on the journey. What was in those sandwiches I shall never know, but they were perfectly horrible and inedible. The infamous snoek perhaps, a substitute fish for the starving war-workers, or spam, or corned beef, or reconstituted egg. This was the only refreshment or sustenance offered us, but though our spirits were a little dashed, we talked and laughed and looked forward to our arrival in Czechoslovakia.

Four hours later, at three o'clock, the aircraft landed at Prague Airport, and after the formal presentations, to the President of Czechoslovakia, Dr Benes, and the Foreign Minister, Dr Masaryk, we were taken to our hotel, where straight away we ordered tea. We were gaspingly thirsty and very hungry, having eaten and drunk nothing at all since breakfast in our own homes many hours earlier.

The smiling Czech waiter at the hotel looked crestfallen and shook his head. There was no tea whatsoever in Prague, he told us regretfully. But, as a very great favour, he would bring us some *real* coffee.

Real coffee! None of us could remember what real coffee was like. It had been unobtainable throughout the war years. When the silver tray arrived, carried with great ceremony by the waiter and bearing a silver coffee-pot and porcelain cups and saucers, the coffee was poured out for us and we thankfully seized our cups and sipped the liquid. It was absolutely revolting. Ersatz coffee. So off we trooped upstairs to change in our rooms with yawningly empty stomachs. Dinner was promised to follow before we went to hear Firkusny play.

'Dinner' proved to be a quick snack, so we were all still hungry but could not complain as we were taken on at once to the concert hall for the inaugural concert. Firkusny was to play Martinu's Second Piano Concerto, whose melodic line derived from Moravian folk-music, eleven years after its first performance. The atmosphere was already electric when news came that Martinu had had a serious accident and was unable to be present.

Czechoslovakia, a land-locked country which produced amazing genius, had emerged from the oppressive years of occupation with an extraordinary buoyancy. The ovation accorded their young pianist before he had played even one note was stupendous. No one can imagine the emotion and euphoria he evoked in the audience. At the end of the concert the audience could not be contained. They all mounted the platform and crowded round him as he sat at the piano, clamouring for an encore, so there was hardly room for him to move his arms. He played one, then two, then three encores, and still the audience was insatiable. He played three more encores and then the yawning attendants, desperate to go home, put out the lights. Firkusny played a seventh encore. Still the audience would not leave the stage, let alone the hall, so the attendants pushed their way through the throng and tried to close down the piano. But the audience began to scuffle with the attendants, refusing to let the piano-lid be lowered, and Firkusky played an eighth encore in semi-darkness in a rapt silence from audience and attendants alike. I was myself most affected by this terrific demonstration of affection by the crowd for their fellow-countryman.

The party following the concert was hosted by the young, brilliant, popular Kubelik, and his wife, not only a charming hostess but a fine violinist herself. Kubelik's father, the famous violinist Jan Kubelik, had been the son of a Czech gardener, and known in his time as having earned more money than any other living soloist, invested in beautiful castles, which he restored to their original grandeur.

The British concerts were to follow, conducted by Sir Adrian Boult. Under his baton I was to play the John Ireland Piano Concerto. My solo recital was to follow two days later.

Whether it was malnutrition added to excitement and emotion I do not know, but the day after I had played the John Ireland I woke up in the hotel feeling ill and with a sore throat. A doctor was summoned and took my temperature: it was 101, and tonsillitis was diagnosed. The next evening I was due to give my solo recital and I would not, could not, cancel it. I was dosed up and stayed in bed. From my hotel window my feverish eyes had for the first time since my arrival in Prague an opportunity to contemplate the view. The morning sun lit up with extraordinary clarity the red and gold and green roof-scape of domes and spires, while beyond, my eyes were led to hills clouded with pink and white May blossom. Prague had a tangible ambience of courage and genius and holiness. One could feel it.

I felt really ill but in the late afternoon I began to get ready for my recital. I had chosen to wear a simple, draped, white jersey dress. For the first half of my programme I had selected a mixture of classics, ending with the brilliant Ravel Toccata which closes *Le Tombeau de Couperin*. When I finished I was bathed in perspiration and could hardly totter off the stage to the tumultuous applause. I could see Rafael Kubelik, tall and beautiful, standing in the wings clapping away.

In England it is not usual for artists to give encores, or extras as they are called in the United States, during an interval. But the audience would not let me go. Kubelik pushed me, dazed as I was, back on the stage. 'Go on!' he urged me excitedly, so, bemused with fever and the bright lights blinding my eyes, I sat down again at the piano and began to play the Chopin Waltz in G Flat, a piece I knew backwards, which I could play in my sleep, so many hundreds of times had I played it. But I really was not ready and did not quite know where I was; I should have been resting in my dressing-room, preparing for the second half of my programme. To my horror I had a 'block', lost the 'chain', and could not think what came next in this all-too-familiar piece of music. I managed to play the next bit quite happily, then the 'block' came again and by then I was terribly upset and hardly knew what I was doing. I finished as best as I could and rushed off the stage, my head bowed in shame at what I had done, to the artists' room.

Kubelik came in still clapping enthusiastically, to find me collapsed on the dressing-table, my head in my arms, weeping uncontrollably and crying: 'I'm finished! I'm finished! My career is finished!'

Kubelik exhorted me to go on again. The audience were still applauding, clamouring for my return. I wiped my face, powdered my nose and stood up. And as I left the dressing-room I began humming the waltz to myself as I went. 'How does the ruddy thing go?' I murmured exasperatedly. On the stage I bowed to the audience, then I sat down and played the Chopin waltz all over again, this time perfectly, to even greater applause.

And the fifty-three-minute Dale Sonata I played also without any mistakes!

The next day at the hotel, despite my performance the previous night, my sore throat and temperature, I went to the hotel hairdresser. The young hair-stylist greeted me with knowing laughter. 'You're not the little English girl who pretended to forget her Chopin last night, are you?' He and the other *cognoscenti* thought my only too-real lapse of memory was a huge practical joke. The press alluded to

Kubelik and myself as 'Rafael and the Angel', on account of my white gown.

After that I stayed in bed, only getting up to hear the Russians play. I could not possibly miss them, for Lev Oborin was to play the Khachaturian Piano Concerto. Khachaturian had dedicated this work to Oborin,[1] a winner of the Russian Chopin Competition and a superb teacher at the Moscow Conservatoire. Oborin and I had both recorded the piano concerto and when we met after the concert we embraced each other enthusiastically and agreed to exchange recordings of this masterpiece with which we had been so intimately connected.

These two crucial visits overseas, to Paris and Prague, were the forerunners of innumerable cultural missions I went on for Britain. I was one of the first British pianists to tour the USSR after the war. It was my destiny to give the fantastic Khachaturian Concerto its first performance in London, Paris, La Scala, Milan, Brussels and Australia.

In 1948 my agent at last arranged for me to make my début in the United States. It was a continent I knew only from movies and I eagerly looked forward to playing at the Town Hall, New York. My husband Colin had been to America and had not liked it; he announced that he would be unable to come with me, as he could not leave his business for so long. He knew I would have a very strenuous time, and also a nerve-wracking one, but I assured him I would be all right.

For this vitally important trip, when I would be without Colin's support, I took along Edna, a very nice Englishwoman, to be my 'helpmate'. The British Inland Revenue generously allowed the employment of such a person to count as 'expenses'.

Quite why I never knew, but to my great sorrow all my little ducklings on the pond in the garden behind my cottage at Oxshott died that spring. I was told the water

---

[1]Ashkenazy was a pupil of Oborin.

was stagnant. Someone had once said to me that the duck is a symbol of love and fidelity in China, and I felt this was an omen. However, I put this at the back of my mind as I prepared for my momentous journey. Colin and I practised regularly.

I was thirty-two when I arrived in the United States, where I was met by a barrage of journalists and photographers who made a great fuss of me, apparently surprised that I should be young and not bad-looking. One of the blasé New York photographers called out at the press conference: 'Give us a leg picture!'

'I'm a concert pianist,' I protested. 'Not a showgirl.'

By then, the autumn of 1948, the New Look created by Christian Dior was all the rage. The short, knee-length skirts of wartime were out, and the ensemble I was wearing was full-skirted and fell in generous folds to my ankles. However, I responded to the journalist's demand and raised my skirts to my knees.

'Lady,' exclaimed the pressman admiringly. 'Those ain't no piano-legs neither!'

For my performance at the New York Town Hall I duly wore my Nina Ricci dress. At the interval of the recital Sol Hurok, who was presenting me, together with Agnes de Mille and her husband Walter Prude, came round to the dressing-room and when the bell rang to warn me to be ready to go on stage again, I turned to Edna, my 'helpmate', and said: 'Oh, Edna, can I please have my bottle?'

Walter Prude looked horrified and said in a shocked voice: 'You're not going to *drink*?'

'No, no, Walter,' I explained, laughing. 'My hot-water bottle for my hands.'

I do like to make sure my hands are warm before I play. If my hands are cold, the muscles will not work and respond properly. My heart is warm, too, if my hands are warm. During the war I had got into the habit of carrying a white fur muff in which I tucked my hands and a baby-sized hot-water bottle as I walked the sometimes long distances between the dressing-room and the stage, handing it to my helpmate or a stage-hand in the wings before stepping out on to the platform.

The next day, 25 November 1948, Noel Straus wrote in *The New York Times*: 'The handsome, modest musician at once established herself as an artist of decided importance, both as technician and interpreter.' Straus went on to say he had never heard Ravel's Toccata performed with such 'spontaneity or any comparable exquisiteness of tinting or finesse . . . an artist of keen insight and superb pianistic attainments'.

My programme had consisted of:

Bach-Busoni's Toccata in C Major
Mendelssohn's *Variations Sérieuses*
Chopin's Scherzo in C Sharp Minor
Brahms's Variations on a Theme of Paganini, Bk II

INTERVAL

Ravel's Ondine and Toccata
Rachmaninov's Preludes in D Flat, G Flat, and B Flat
Liszt's *Jeux d'Eaux à La Villa d'Este*
Liszt's Polonaise in E Major

At one of the private recitals I was seated at the piano, having just played, and not thinking of anything in particular, when a young man a little taller than myself, wearing horn-rimmed glasses behind which shone a pair of lively brown eyes, came up to me at the piano. 'Can I get you something to eat?' he asked. It was true I was hungry after my performance and the food in America was marvellous after the years of privation in England during and after the war. 'I'm Bennet Korn,' he told me, handing me a plate of excellent canapés. He worked in radio.

We seemed to have a great deal to talk about together and as we left that party a friend remarked to me: 'That young American is not going to forget you.'

Nor did he. He quickly got in touch with me and soon he was taking me out and showing me his New York: Central Park; the Bronx, the Statue of Liberty. It was a marvellous city, so vital, young and modern, as was my guide. We dined and danced together every night till the early hours. Bennet adored all kinds of music and had a superb collection of records, classical and jazz. He also played the saxophone really well. He was so quick, so brilliant, with a darting, lively intelligence. It was said he was the best salesman in New York, working for a time on commercial radio. I fell head over heels in love with him and he with me.

Bennet had never been married; he lived alone in a large, one-room apartment, but was devoted to his parents and his sister, who were Orthodox Jews living in Brooklyn. He was born in Austria and had arrived with his family in the United States when he was seven. He too was in love for the first time and with a devout Roman Catholic Englishwoman who was married and shortly returning to her husband. Any future for us seemed remote, but we agreed that I should ask Colin for a divorce and return as soon possible to New York, when we would get married.

On my return to England I was excited and keyed up. What had happened between Bennet and myself had seemed to be so natural: we were the same age and I had immediately been attracted to him and he to me. I decided I must tell my husband that Bennet and I were in love and wished to spend the rest of our lives together, and ask him to release me from our marriage, as he had promised to do. Now, suddenly, everything had changed. On my first night home, Colin was faced no longer by a meek and retiring, obedient young wife, but with a mature woman passionately in love with a man of her own age. Afterwards we went to our separate rooms.

The following morning I rose and breakfasted alone before going straight to the music-room for my practice. It was lunch-time before I realized that I had seen no sign of Colin nor heard any sound from his room. I knocked on the door but there was no reply. I went in. He was still in bed asleep, and when I touched him he did not stir. Very frightened I called the doctor, who came at once and found that Colin had taken an overdose of sleeping-tablets. An ambulance came and took him away.

Deeply shocked by Colin's attempted suicide, I resolved that if he survived, it was my duty to stay with him. I told Bennet that all was over between us, and Colin and I continued to live together.

It must be said that, after the excitement, vitality and interest of going to America, life in Surrey seemed somewhat flat. Inevitably I felt a sense of anticlimax. Colin and I resumed our dual practising for my recitals and concerts, but as I saw my women friends' growing young families I felt even more keenly the deprivation of children to call my own. Also, by the time the decade ended, my husband Colin, who had seemed not so very much older than myself at the time of our marriage ten years earlier, had aged a good deal. He was now seventy-two while I was thirty-four.

This uncomfortable situation went on for months. Bennet and I continued to correspond and to telephone each other. I even had a severe attack of dermatitis, which was diagnosed as psychosomatic, so great was my longing to be with Bennet. At last I could stand it no longer. Nine months later I told Colin I must go to Bennet, and Colin then agreed to a divorce. The painful negotiations were arranged with discretion and, to our relief, without publicity. Recklessly disregarding my own interests, I let Colin keep the house at Oxshott.

Ironically, during this unhappy period of his life, Colin met a young woman in London who asked him why he looked so miserable. 'My wife has gone off with an American,' Colin told her, whereupon apparently the young woman proposed to him. (That, at least was Colin's story.) In due course they married and she bore him a son.

As soon as I could arrange it, I flew to New York for what I thought would be my wedding. On arrival I found Bennet as magnetically attractive and charming as ever, and he felt the

ve)
Robert Limpenny
ıt)
ıra aged one year eleven months

(*left*)
Captain John Johnstone
(*above*)
Beatrice Limpenny

Joseph Johnstone

ght)
bias Matthay, 'Uncle Tobs'
elow)
oura with M. Edmond Jaminé,
arling Bonpapa'

(*left*)
Moura at the Convent piano, Tongres

Moura aged twenty-one, photographed by Queen Elisabeth of Belgium

(*left*)
Relaxing while on a concert tour in Canada
(*below*)
Moura with Aram Khachaturian, New York

Moura with Sir Adrian Boult

(r

Moura with her nephew, Christopher Johns

Moura with Queen Elizabeth the Queen Mother and Princess Margaret after a concert at the Fermoy Centre, King's Lynn

(*above*)
The Prince of Wales with Moura at the Royal Festival Hall, 1979
(*right*)
Prince Louis de Polignac

same way about me. But he had not found the courage to tell his mother he wanted to marry me. He was simply terrified his mother would veto the marriage. He was thirty-five but still very much a 'mother's boy'.

It was quite a crisis for me, since I had crossed the Atlantic for him, having left my husband and divorced him. In consternation and rage I waited, day after day, as Bennet procrastinated, and finally I turned on him and told him I was returning to London. I meant what I said and caught the next plane for a humiliating return.

No sooner had I arrived back in London in a state of fury and despair at my rejection, than the telephone rang. It was Bennet, all remorse, begging forgiveness, and confessing his realization that he adored me and could not live without me.

In the summer of 1951 I was engaged to play at the Proms. Two days before my concert I met Bennet at the airport and we were ecstatically reunited. We obtained a special licence and made all the arrangements to be married at Chelsea Registry Office the morning of the concert. Wearing white, with Bennet's white roses pinned to my bag, I drove to Chelsea in a white Rolls-Royce. Afterwards, I had to rush off to rehearsal at noon. As I went into the auditorium, the orchestra, conducted by none other than Basil Cameron, got to their feet and played the Wedding March. After the rehearsal Bennet and I went to the Savoy for a wedding breakfast, but I could not drink any champagne, for I was playing that night. It was one of my favourite concerti, the Beethoven Fourth, and I played to a marvellous reception. I was ecstatically happy.

Concert engagements in the north of England followed, and then Bennet and I flew to New York to start our married life together.

When we reached New York I asked Bennet how his mother had reacted to the news that he was coming to

London to marry me. Bennet confessed that he had not dared to tell her.

Fury possessed me. I raged at him, seized the telephone and put the receiver into his hand. 'Ring her and tell her at once!' I said.

Bennet was literally trembling from head to foot as he dialled. I could hear his mother's voice quite clearly.

'I . . . I've got something to tell you, Mom,' he began shakily. 'I've married Moura.'

'Why didn't you tell me?' replied Mrs Korn sweetly. 'I could have come over to London for the wedding. After all, you are my only son.'

Bennet had been making his mother an allowance, which he now considered discontinuing, but I would not allow this. In fact, Mrs Korn told her friends that she greatly approved of her daughter-in-law, because she herself went to Brooklyn once a month to give her, Mrs Korn, her son's allowance.

Soon I found myself caught up in a whirlwind life which revolved round Bennet's new job in television. At first we lived in his apartment; a grand piano, lots of records and his saxophone filled the small space. Bennet was a dynamic man of diverse talents which he quickly channelled into numerous bewildering directions. He became president of thirteen television companies all over the United States. He said to me once: 'In America, we sell. In England, you just make things available.' He had a brilliant mind and was the first man to bring culture to television in New York. And he bought programmes from the BBC.

It seemed that my longing for a child was at last to be realized. When I became pregnant, I joyfully prepared a lavish layette in the nursery of our new, larger apartment, and engaged a Scottish nanny who came over from England and settled in prior to the birth.

Our first child, a son, was stillborn. My wretchedness no words can describe. The young Scottish nanny was so sweet to me. We begged her to stay on for a while, she was such a comfort, before seeing her off back to England.

I became pregnant again and all my hopes for a child were revived once more. This time twins were diagnosed and there seemed no medical or physiological reason why they should not be carried full term. Inexplicably, however, twin boys were born prematurely, at Christmas time, weighing 2½ pounds each, but they did not survive. I became pregnant for a third time and at first all seemed to be going well. Then it appeared that the baby was very small and I was warned by my obstetrician that I might not carry it full term. As the months passed my hopes were raised and at last a son was born at 8½ months. But he was very small, weighing less than 4 pounds, and was put into an incubator immediately. We named him Charles Joseph after my brother who had been killed in the war. Soon after the birth Bennet and I went down to the nursery to see our son. Behind the glass wall of the incubator he looked very frail. He was sleeping. Then suddenly to my surprise and joy he opened his eyes and looked straight at me. It was a moment I shall never forget. Thirty-five hours after his birth he died.

I cried a great deal after that. Back in our apartment I would talk about our son with Bennet. And then one day, I said to him: 'Let's not talk about the baby any more because crying won't bring him back.' I turned the page and it was the end of the chapter.

About this time we were invited by Sir Harold and Lady Mitchell to Jamaica where I could recuperate and Bennet have a much-needed rest. Lady Mitchell was very touched by the concerned way Bennet looked at me – so affectionately, she said. Jamaica was lush and romantic, a paradise after the hectic New York schedule my husband kept. We were invited to dinner by Noël Coward. It was unforgettable. After dinner Noël turned to me and said in his inimitable staccato tone: 'Now Moura, you and I are going to play my two pianos.' He led me to one and I sat down while he went to the other.

'Where's the music?' I asked bewilderedly.

'I have no music,' explained Noël succinctly.

'How are we going to play if we have no music?' I demanded, laughing.

'I cannot read music,' confessed Noël.

'I cannot improvise,' I admitted.

'Never mind,' said Noël. 'We'll improvise together.'

So Noël strummed a few chords adorably while I at the other piano stumbled along as best I could, trying to copy and follow him, to the great entertainment of the rest of the party.

Fira Benenson, who as a little girl in St Petersburg had been taught English by my mother, had established her own couture house in New York. Her dress designs were gorgeous and she made several concert gowns for me. I had never given up playing the piano or practising. When Khachaturian came to London to conduct a concert of his works, Oistrakh was to play the Oistrakh violin concerto and I was engaged to play again the piano concerto. It was really frightening. Khachaturian was a tall, burly figure with smouldering black eyes and an expressive mouth. He was wonderful because he just took me along with him. He was so full of fire, of passion. He wrote on my music: 'Like a tank approaching, like a tigress.' It was absolutely fantastic. I never played the piano concerto so well again as with him, because he conducted it so powerfully and he took me along with him.

Bennet and I used to rent a house on Long Island to escape the pressures and heat of New York summers, and as I have always loved the country I persuaded Bennet to let me find a holiday house and weekend retreat of our own on Long Island. To the agent I said: 'Find me something unusual. Something no one else wants.'

When we told Bennet's mother, she said: 'Don't buy a cheap little house. Buy a better house, it will increase in value.'

This was how we came to buy 'the doll's house', in Locust Valley, one hour and five minutes from New York. We called it the doll's house because everything in it was tiny. Apart from one large bedroom, there were two other tiny bedrooms, two small kitchens and two bathrooms. I had great fun arranging it. Behind the house, four acres of land went down to the sea, Mill Neck Bay. It was idyllic. We acquired a beautiful Siamese cat called Suki. We were a very happy and successful young couple with lots of friends in many spheres, including the United Nations, and there was no conflict in our separate worlds of classical music and television. Bennet's last boss was the brilliant John Kluge. Music was my work. I preferred to keep it quite apart from my personal and social life, and disliked talking about it. Very few of my friends, then and now, are musical or know anything at all about music. I had so many other interests that my friends did not have to be musical.

At first I had been very shy of my husband's hectic life-style. His colleagues were all fast-talking, dynamic executives like himself, and I could not keep up with them at all. He would take me to parties and I was completely tongue-tied. Bennet told me this was because all I could think of was myself and my shyness. He was an expert at public relations. 'Don't think of yourself,' he told me. 'Think of the other person and say something of interest to that person straight away. It puts the onus on that person.'

That helped me enormously and I completely lost my shyness, so that now I never mind going anywhere alone. Many of my women friends won't go anywhere without an escort, but this does not bother me at all.

In 1956 I made an epic journey to Czechoslovakia again, and to Russia, to play with the London Philharmonic Orchestra. I gave seven concerts, five in Moscow and two in Leningrad. How would my mother have reacted to the grey drabness and uniformity I found there? I had never been to Leningrad, the great city my mother and aunts had known and loved so well as St Petersburg in the years before the First World War. It was still a beautiful city.

In Moscow at one of the social events I was to meet Mr Andrei Gromyko and I wondered what on earth I could find to say to this great diplomat; he had been much loved at the United Nations. My husband's advice came in useful, for when we came face to face, I burst out:'Oh! Mr Gromyko I think we have a lot of friends in common at the United Nations.' At once we were talking away quite happily.

Before leaving America for this trip I had given a copy of the itinerary to Bennet, who was rather worried about my going behind the Iron Curtain, together with a list of the hotels where I was to stay. Bennet telephoned one of the hotels, to be told I was not there, had not been there and was not expected. This threw him into a panic. Where was I? Stories that came out of Russia activated his imagination. Had I been abducted? Had I been sent to Siberia? Was I in a Russian gaol? He kept on telephoning the hotel, to be met by a stone wall of negativity.

One of Bennet's close friends was the great advertising man, Rosser Reeves. Also a brilliant chess player, Reeves had not long returned from Soviet Russia where he had gone as president of a chess team. In Russia he had met Nikita Khrushchev and the two men had hit it off tremendously well. So Bennet telephoned his friend for advice. 'I can't find Moura!' he told Rosser Reeves. 'What shall I do?' 'Send Khrushchev a telegram' was the reply.

So Bennet worded a telegram to the effect that his wife, a soloist with the London Philharmonic Orchestra, must be located, since he needed to contact her at once. This had an immediate result. Bennet learned that the hotels we were booked into had been changed and I was staying at a different one.

That night at supper after the concert, the last in Moscow, Adrian Boult, a formidably tall, balding figure with a moustache, who at times reminded me of my first husband Colin, and my Uncle Bede, was cutting and sarcastic. 'Your husband has been in touch with Khrushchev,' he said severely. 'When we get to England I suppose he'll be ringing the Queen next to find out where you are there!'

I felt mortified. I put my head on my arms and wept bitterly into my plate. I felt I had disgraced my country. Then the representative from the Soviet Ministry of Culture touched me gently on the shoulder. 'Why are you crying?' he asked.

I told him. 'My husband sent a telegram to Mr Khrushchev,' I sobbed. 'He couldn't find me. I've let my country down. It's a terrible disgrace.' And I began to weep again.

'Wipe your tears away,' he counselled me, smiling. 'You have such pretty eyes.' I stopped crying and gazed at this kindly Communist. 'We Russians understand love. Your husband loves you and was trying to find you, that's all.'

I got on wonderfully with the Russians and wondered again if I had any Russian blood. After all, my Austrian great-grandfather had lived not far from the Russian border. Another thought struck me. Had my mother been 'good' in Leningrad all those years ago before her marriage? I had not inherited the long straight, Wellington nose my brothers possessed, but a short nose, a Russian nose, so I had been told. But I had the Johnstone eyes. And I remembered that I had been born a year after my parents married.

I decided I was tired of being pigeon-holed as a virtuoso. I went for some lessons to Edward Steuermann, that marvellous musician who was a pupil of Schoenberg and gave all the first performances of Schoenberg's music. His was a completely different approach from Matthay. He was a tremendous brain, a great stickler for what was written, Germanic and classical. 'You never know a piece till you come back to it the third time,' Matthay had said.

I used to get very depressed when I could not do what I wanted to do even though I practised and practised, and inexplicably a few months later I would return to the same piece to find the difficulties had disappeared. A psychologist explained to me that the work I had done had been absorbed into the subconscious and I could now play the piece as I wished quite effortlessly.

With Edward Steuermann I worked on Beethoven's 'Emperor' Concerto. Steuermann wanted me to play the six short pieces from Schoenberg's Op. 19. Feeling it essential that I should understand their theoretical bases, he offered a detailed explanation of their motivic and atonal construction, their dependence on hexachordal relationships. This meant little or nothing to me from a musical standpoint. Steuermann saw that I was puzzled and finally advised me: 'Moura, when you go home and work on these, play them as though they were Rachmaninov.'

I took his advice. That is, I tried to make them very musical and melodious, and phrased them as Matthay had taught me.

When I came back and played them to Steuermann he was absolutely thrilled. 'Don't change them. It's fine,' he said. So I played them at my recital the following year and they were received so enthusiastically, they were almost more successful than anything else in my repertoire.

In 1956 I went to play in Prague. Although I was married to an American I still retained my British citizenship and passport, but I had a green card, a so-called 'alien's' resident's card. I broke my journey to play at the Royal Festival Hall in a charity concert in aid of the Kathleen Ferrier Appeal. To my surprise, on arrival at Prague I found picture postcards of myself on sale in all the shops, reproducing a photograph taken especially for my earlier visit.

On my return to New York I received a severe grilling by the US immigration authorities. What countries had I been to?

'Czechoslovakia,' I replied, and at once was regarded with great suspicion. It seemed I had gone there without the permission of the US State Department. Fruitlessly I pointed out that I was a British subject and that it had all been arranged by my agent, Ibbs and Tillett. The United States had had nothing to do with it.

'Lady, you're in trouble!' I was told succinctly. I feared I would be sent back to England at once and not allowed to go to my own home in New York. 'Wait!' ordered the officer.

I waited and waited and waited and at last was instructed to attend the immigration office between 8 and 9 a.m. in a few days' time to be interrogated by a security officer. Was I about to be sent to Ellis Island? In the meantime *The New York Times* came out, and there was my photograph with Bennet on the front page beneath a headline and report of the great success Moura Lympany had had behind the Iron Curtain as a cultural ambassadress!

I spent the whole day waiting in an office with lots of other people. I sat there from the hour of my arrival at 8 a.m. and by 4 p.m. I was bored and angry at having my time wasted. I had concerts to practise for, my household to attend to, my husband to be reunited with. 'Could I be seen now?' I pleaded.

I was directed to a cubicle and sat before a desk, behind which sat the interrogating officer. 'Where have you been?' he demanded.

'Prague.'

'Where did you stay?'

'The British Embassy.'

'How long for?'

'Two weeks, on and off.'

'Where else did you go?'

'Other towns outside Prague.'

'Did you speak to or see any Czechs?'

'Of course!'

'What did you speak about?' he demanded sternly.

'Well, at a dinner-party I sat next to a charming Czech. What did we speak about?' I paused. 'We spoke about love.'

My interrogator sat up. 'You spoke to a Communist about love!' he shouted furiously.

'What else would a man and a woman speak about at a dinner-party?' I asked innocently.

My interrogator stood up and glared at me. 'I must telephone Washington at once.' He left the cubicle and I could hear him repeating our conversation down the telephone. Then he returned, sat down, and glared again at me. 'You can go!' he ordered.

All these years my father and mother had lived somewhat separate lives. My mother had lived on at Rosemont in Yelverton, her lively mind active to the end. She was teaching herself Hungarian when she died, to be buried in Plymouth. The house was bequeathed to her brothers, with the proviso that my father be allowed to live in it for the rest of his life. This was because my mother felt she must repay all the help her brothers had given her, particularly concerning her sons' education. So my father lived on at Rosemont in his retirement. He was quite unchanged and the stories told of him were legion. He was as upright in his bearing as ever and still as charming. He lived in one room in the house, let out the rest as bed-sitters, and every day, immaculately dressed, strolled to the local hotel for lunch, where he was a great attraction as a raconteur. Once he believed he had won the pools, ordered champagne for all the habitués of the hotel, only to discover later that he had scored one point too little and had not won at all. He was quite good-humoured about it.

He still played golf and tennis although he was in his late seventies. His devoted friends Sylvia and Don Witts played with him, drove him about, and he spent every Christmas and Easter with them and their children. They lived only four minutes' walk from Rosemont. Sylvia and Don were a public-spirited couple. She was a magistrate, chairman of the District Council, and president of the Yelverton Women's Institute, while Don was chairman and finance director of the Royal Horticultural Society. Captain Johnstone – 'Johnnie', as my father was known – was a keen sportsman and regularly umpired local cricket matches. Sylvia would cook cottage pies he could heat up in his Baby Belling cooker. They went to point-to-points together at Newton Abbot and my father, a distinguished, soldierly figure in blazer or tweeds, smoking Erinmore in a briar pipe, was well known all over North Devon. He loved animals and once found an owl with a broken wing, nursed it back to health, digging worms for it every day and building a small cage for it outside the back door of Rosemont. He would go out walking, the owl perched on his shoulder. When it was well enough to fly, he set it free.

Once at a convivial lunch-time session at the Rick Hotel, my father met a man who had that morning with a spinner caught a ten-pound salmon in the Burrator Reservoir. Nothing would deter my father. He called for a taxi to take him to Tavistock, bought a spinner in the fishing-tackle shop, and on he went in the taxi to the reservoir where, fortunately, he asked the taxi-driver to wait for him. My father promptly fell into the reservoir and had to be rescued by the taxi-driver.

When he was in his late seventies, I arranged for my father to travel from Southampton on the *Queen Mary* to stay with us in New York. I sent him his ticket and plenty of cash to spend. Unfortunately there was a dock strike at the time and so the passengers were instructed to make their way to Liverpool. On arrival at Liverpool my father boarded the ship and found his cabin, which he was to share with another passenger.

I shall never know the truth of what happened. Tired after his unexpected journey to Liverpool, my father fell asleep in his berth and on awaking found his wallet, containing all the cash I had sent him, was missing. He was forced to wire me for more.

When he finally arrived looking tanned and handsome and charming as ever we all had a wonderful time together. The Americans adored him, so English was he in every way, and I was glad I had been able to give him this happy holiday in the United States with me and my husband.

For my father's eightieth birthday, Bennet and I travelled to England where Sylvia and Don Witts had organized a birthday-party at the Links Hotel. For the occasion I proudly wore a suit tailored in the Johnstone tartan of grey-blue and sage-green with a yellow stripe. About forty guests came, and after dinner, at Sylvia's request, I sat at the hotel's upright piano to play Debussy's *Clair de Lune*. Sylvia told me afterwards that at once all the merry chatter ceased and there was total silence. Those in the public bar, on hearing the first notes, also fell silent and gradually they trickled out to join our party and listen to Debussy.

A most entertaining artist was present, and when he invited us all to go to his studio, Don, Sylvia, my father and Bennet and I piled into Don's car and off we went to look at his pictures. The studio was a ramshackle hut in the middle of nowhere with a ladder leading upstairs, climbed with difficulty by my eighty-year-old father, now rather tired after the excitement of his birthday-party. The artist produced jam jars and opened a bottle of Scotch whisky.

I liked the artist's work, huge splashy abstracts, and decided one large canvas would look marvellous in our Long Island doll's house. So I bought it. Don agreed to crate it and send it to me in America.

'Which way up should it go?' I asked naïvely.

'This way,' said my father authoritatively. 'The paint drips run downwards.'

It had been a marvellous birthday-party. Don, my father's devoted friend, duly drove him home and saw him safely into bed.

The following year, Sylvia Witts was passing Rosemont one day when she noticed the curtains were still drawn. My father was ill. I happened to be in England at the time, so I immediately telephoned Emmie Tillett and most unusually cancelled a concert. 'My father is in hospital,' I explained.

'But he's not really your father, is he?' asked Emmie.

'Of course he is!' I exclaimed. Because I had assumed my mother's maiden name, and to facilitate hotel and travelling had had it made official by deed poll, so that it was on my passport, she believed I was illegitimate.

My father had cancer of the liver. I was told it might have begun twenty years ago and that there was now no hope for him. He was moved into a large private room with a second bed where I could stay and be with him in the hospital till he died. He died a few days later, and was buried next to my mother in the cemetery at Plymouth.

# 44 Bruton Place, Mayfair

Ten wonderful years had passed since Bennet and I had married. Our life together was cloudless. There was no warning that shortly I was to enter on a long and painful period of my life.

All this time I had given concerts in the United States but had resisted most blandishments and pressures from my agents Ibbs and Tillett to tour overseas. Finally I did agree to the persuasions of Emmie Tillett, managing director of the firm and a personal friend, to absent myself from my adored husband and go to Australia. I was to be away for five weeks.

Before such tours artists engaged are sent a booklet, for considerable preparation and planning is essential some time in advance, quite apart from the musical programme itself. The public is unaware of this. Itineraries are made by the tour promoters, hotels are researched and booked, and we, the performers, are expected to familiarize ourselves and adhere to what has been arranged for us. 'The standard of Australian hotel accommodation has improved enormously in recent years,' I was assured, 'both in the capital cities and main provincial centres. Modern hotels now cater for the most fastidious tastes.' Australian hotels were often far better than British ones.

I could be playing as many as twenty-five different

composers, which meant a large amount of sheet music. I preferred to carry this separately from my other luggage. I needed it with me to study on the journey, and also I was afraid of losing it and felt it was safer in my hands. And the clothes we would be wearing on and off the platform, according to the variations in weather and climate, also amounted to a great deal of weighty luggage. 'A woman artist owning a fur coat should bring it with her if she is to arrive after mid-March,' I was advised.

We were warned not to overlook arranging a visa for the return journey. There were three types of visas: (1) transit, (2) visitor's and (3) working. Five to six weeks' notice was necessary for any trips to India or the Philippines, Japan or the USSR.

My contract provided for the fare to be paid by the Australian Broadcasting Commission, and I must not perform for any other management without first seeking permission from the ABC. And any 'en route' engagements would mean a proportion of the fee would be due to ABC by the management concerned.

Directly the contract had been signed, photographs and publicity material must be forwarded, for the media planners arrange printing and press conferences months ahead. 'No old photographs, please, and photographs that you would rather we did not use. . . . We need the best you can give us.' So sittings with photographers had to be booked, hair and make-up and clothes organized for them first. It will be seen that, music apart, the preparation required all my time and attention. Any unauthorized change in the programme cost us 10 per cent of the fee. 'Programme changes irritate concert audiences,' we were told, 'and mar broadcasts. Recital programmes which are performed several times must be carefully rationed to avoid overmuch repetition.'

On my return journey from Australia on an earlier visit (in 1948, I think, when I was still married to Colin Defries) the flying-boat landed at Surabaya, where the second pilot took over and prepared to take off again for Singapore. My seat was next to a window which looked out over one of the flying-boat's wings. When the aircraft turned, prior to taking off, its engines revving up violently and very loudly, I saw to my horror that on the 'turn' the pilot had not kept the aircraft level and the one float on my side was, instead of above the water, submerged, beating against the water trying to get free. 'The float's gone!' I screamed above the deafening roar of engines.

One of the officers came running to the passengers to instruct us what to do. We were to take off our shoes and climb out of the emergency exits. 'Follow me!' he called.

I was nearest to the door and shot out, to find myself on a perpendicular wing high in the air. I said to him: 'Put your arms around me!' My stockinged feet had no hold on the surface and I was sliding down it.

'I haven't any pants on!' replied the man. He had taken off his trousers and was wearing only his underpants.

'I don't care what you've got on,' I screamed, 'I can't swim and there are sharks down there!'

We clung on to the wing of the crippled flying-boat for some time. No one dared come near us for fear any attempt to right the flying-boat would tip it fatally into the sea. We were taken off just in time, to see the aircraft turn turtle and sink before our eyes.

I never saw my shoes again and all the crew's luggage was lost – but ours was recovered. When we reached Singapore there were amazing reports in the newspapers, headlined: 'SLIGHT MISHAP TO FLYING-BOAT. There was a slight mishap to the flying-boat coming to Singapore yesterday, but after a certain time it was able to take off.' And it was at the bottom of the sea!

On my first night home in New York after being away on what had seemed an unconscionably long journey, Bennet pressed me to go to a party to be given for the great Spanish painter Salvador Dali by a young friend of Bennet's, a girl in her twenties. I learned afterwards that our hostess had decided a few weeks earlier that it was time for her to settle down and marry. She had two men in mind, one of whom was my husband, Bennet. During my absence in Australia she had made a dead set at him and had in fact seduced him. Never had I dreamed this could happen to me. I had felt utterly secure. Suddenly my world was shattered. For twenty years I had been cherished – first by Colin, then by Bennet. Now I was cast out into a terrible abyss, a wilderness without direction. I was lost and alone, in an apartment on East 68th Street.

Fortunately I had many friends so I was not entirely abandoned. At one party I met a member of the overseas *corps diplomatique*, a charming, cultured man seven and a half years older than myself. He, too, was going through a very difficult personal crisis, more tragic than mine, for his wife had recently committed suicide. We fell in love with each other on the rebound, and although our friendship continued for over a year, there seemed to be no real future in it for either of us. But our involvement had helped to heal our respective wounds and we remained friends.

It was not easy, either, for me to pick up the threads of my career, which had played a secondary role in my life since my marriage to Bennet. Americans worship success and the failure of my marriage affected my playing disastrously. I had lost confidence in myself completely and wailed to all my friends that I was finished, personally and professionally.

One of the tender aspects of my life at this time was my growing love for my young nephew and godson, Christopher Johnstone, then in his teens. He had had a difficult childhood, for his parents, my brother Tony and his Austrian wife Dita, had parted, and the boy seemed to be pushed from pillar to post, staying with different people. He came to stay with me and became a great friend. He was musical and artistically sensitive, a charming, attractive and highly intelligent youth.

With me he had a kind of security neither of his parents, either temperamentally, emotionally or materially, was able to give him, and gradually the aunt-nephew relationship evolved into almost a mother-son one. It was the most wonderful balm for me to be lent, as it were, Christopher, to be my surrogate son.

I recall one occasion when he turned up at my apartment just as I was about to set off for a smart wedding reception on Fifth Avenue. He was driving a borrowed car, a terrible old French Citroen 2CV literally falling to pieces and tied up with string. He could have it for 50 dollars, he explained with a hopeful grin. Of course I gave him the money. He offered to drive me to Fifth Avenue and, I thought, why not? Dressed in a mink jacket, jewels, high-heeled shoes and a fabulously pretty hat, I entered the old jalopy, my beloved nephew got in behind the steering-wheel and we both felt like a million dollars.

When the uniformed doorman saw the decrepit vehicle draw up outside his establishment he tried to stop us parking and viewed Christopher with scorn, ordering him to drive on. But Christopher leapt out and ran round the car to escort his Aunt Moura in her finery with great ceremony into the building.

People do not realize that musicians are like actors: we live for our work. Sir John Gielgud gave an address to New York University which taught me a great deal at that long, low point in my life. He said that every artist experiences a 'bad patch'. His 'bad patch' caused him great anguish. He could do nothing right. He had bad reviews for his work, his confidence went, his timing was affected, he began to exaggerate, overact or underplay. He endured and emerged a stronger, better actor than before, finally accepting a minor role and making a great success. Laurence Olivier wrote similarly about his 'bad patch'.

My separation and subsequent divorce from Bennet upset

me unutterably. I seemed to be in a terrifying downward spiral from which only drastic action could pull me back. For nine months I had been in a state of mental suicide. I was not interested in anything whatsoever. The whole point of my life had gone. I did not want to see anyone, practise or anything. My career was going badly. I could see only a few friends, to whom I poured out my misery repeatedly every time we met. Friends can listen for only so long. My doctors gave me sleeping-pills. I didn't care about anything. I told my doctor the only time I was happy was when I took sleeping-pills and forgot my misery. This state of affairs continued for a year or more.

'D'you realize what sleeping-pills do to you?' a Swiss doctor I met at a party asked me. Then he told me: 'They deaden your brain and you won't feel anything any more. If you go on taking pills, your memory will go.'

I considered what he said and decided there was enough love of music left in me for me to appreciate the damage I was inflicting on myself. I went home and threw all the pills down the loo and I have never taken sleeping-pills since. Discipline took over my life. I decided to go back to England. Perhaps, after all, America was not for me.

I had not lived in London since early in the war when I had occupied a small room in Paddington furnished with the bare necessities and an upright piano. But my time in New York married to a high-profile television executive had created a different Moura, a somewhat Americanized one.

In New York I had met the lovely elegant English actress Margaret Leighton, whose short, passionate marriage to the Lithuanian-born actor Laurence Harvey had come to an end. On my occasional visits to England to play, I had rented her house to stay in, preferring the independence it offered to an hotel. It was a mews house in Mayfair: 44 Bruton Place, just off Berkeley Square. She and Laurence Harvey had been idyllically happy in the house. During the war, 44 Bruton Place had been converted into three flats. The top-floor tenant had been the composer of such marvellous songs as 'These Foolish Things'. So inspired was he by Berkeley Square, its lovely leafy trees and, despite the bombing, the nightingales he heard singing there, that he composed 'A Nightingale Sang in Berkeley Square'.[1] Glenn Miller's arrangement of this song was top of the hit parade in the forties. I took on the lease.

Grey skies, grey streets, and the house itself was lugubrious. I must have colour, the sun. I started with a tangerine and lemon Casa Pupo rug, the cheapest rug in London. 'You must decorate how you feel,' said Mr Fleming of Mann and Fleming, the shop I went to for advice. 'It must be an expression of yourself.'

'I want it gay, gay, gay,' I told him, 'a happy house, a lovely atmosphere. A sunny atmosphere.'

Mr Fleming sent me a young designer called Martyn Thomas, who transformed the house. Laurence Harvey's favourite colours were black and purple. The house was almost entirely carpeted in purple, and Doric columns had been erected in several rooms. The dining-room was carpeted in black, and black velvet covered the Jacobean chairs. A black marble table supported by golden eagles dominated the dining-room. Not my style at all.

Emmie Tillett came to see it. Emmie was a Sagittarius. Her brusque manner often frightened people, but she was the kindest, most sympathetic friend, who had spent over thirty years dealing with the foremost artists in the musical world. 'Get rid of this!' she exclaimed. I knew then that she would obtain enough work for me to help pay for the redecoration of the house.

I am an extrovert; I like colours, I like people, I like entertaining. The garage (where, earlier, horses had been stabled) made an excellent reception-room, leading into the music-room (where once carriages were kept), which was

---

[1]Three men are credited with the composition: Jack Strachey, Eric Maschwitz and Manning Sherwin. Which of them lived at 44 Bruton Place is unrecorded.

perfect for large parties. Martyn and I scattered more Spanish Casa Pupo rugs over the floors, while signed portraits of family, friends (including European royal personages) stood on draped tables. A Tunisian bird-cage hung from the ceiling. Poster-hued pictures I had brought back from my tour of Australia brightened up the walls.

Wrought-iron gates led to an almost perpendicular staircase, up which one hauled oneself by means of a rope to the first floor, which had a kitchen and a roof-space that cried out to be made into a patio-garden. More stairs led up to the large drawing-room, along with an en suite bedroom and bathroom.

Martyn's genius made the house beautiful with vibrant colours everywhere. I told him I wanted it to look Cecil Beatonish, but in fact I found, with Martyn to interpret it, my own style. I wanted it to be modern. My bed, shocking pink, was heaped with red fox-fur pelts given to me by a friend. Vermilion and yellow cushions cascaded along three divans with potted palms and tropical plants in the ante-room to the music-room. I wanted to look young and modern too. I put away my gold and diamond wrist-watch and embraced fun-fashion with zest: phosphorescent, lime-green stockings, matching watch-strap, shoes, skirt. With fuchsia and lilac ensembles I wore matching watch-straps and stockings and shoes. I simply adored these lively things and plunged into my new London life with enthusiasm. Edwina Sandys (Mrs Piers Dixon) said: 'Why don't you invite a few of us to your new house?' I told her it wasn't ready. She said that they would be coming to see me, not the house. So I gave my first party. Edwina said to Martyn: 'I don't like it.' Martyn asked her why. She said: 'You come out of the grey sky, the grey street into a Mexican sunshine room.' To which Martyn replied: 'But that is exactly what Moura wants – bright colours, flowers, sunshine!'

However, resuming and developing my career proved no simple matter. The truth was that I had been virtually forgotten by the music world. I had been away too long, a whole new generation of young whizz-kids at the piano had come up, and I was eclipsed. I did not have what most of the young have now: that is, security in myself – self-security or self-confidence.

Despite my determined efforts to fill every hour of every day with activity of every kind, in my solitary moments my thoughts returned again and again to the man I had left behind in New York. About this time I found a beautiful Mercedes 3001D for sale for £200. It was automatic, very big and with a left-hand drive. Nobody wanted it. I consulted my friend and agent Emmie Tillett.

'You buy it, Moura,' she advised, 'and forget that man!'

'How can I forget him?' I wailed.

'You could drive yourself to the country,' Emmie said.

So I bought it and derived enormous pleasure from driving in and out of London. When I gave a party I drove the car out of the garage, and the space was transformed into a reception area.

I could not stand the English weather and nor could I stand the long and miserable English winters. One day I thought that, if I had a greenhouse, I could try to grow things during the winter months and then I would not notice the horrible weather. There was a skylight in the roof of my study and it occurred to me that if one could open it up and reach the flat roof of the adjacent bathroom, one might be able to erect a greenhouse there. I excitedly consulted Martyn. He quickly removed the glass, leant a ladder against the opening, and we both ran up it to see the whole of London spread out below us. Selfridges supplied the greenhouse; electricity and heating were installed, and quite soon I was growing guavas, mangoes and melons, together with passion and other exotic fruits. From my journeys I brought back seeds or cuttings and spent many happy hours working in my greenhouse.

Martyn's speciality was colour co-ordination. Together we discovered the joys of needlework, especially tapestry, Florentine work which was quick, so that in weeks instead of years one could see results. We became really hooked on this, and with his genius Martyn adapted the old seventeenth-century Florentine designs, based on zigzag stitches, sometimes known as Hungarian point or Bargello, into boldly geometric designs. Trellises, diamonds, squares and basket-weave patterns, in heavenly graduating colours, from white through palest apricot to burnt orange, brown and gold and flame. Martyn was very professional in everything he did and ultimately a publisher took him up, which resulted in several books of Martyn's needlework designs being published, illustrated with colour photographs of cushions I had worked.

The rapid technical advances made in transmission and recording greatly affected the music world. Some artists could not cope with the stress of the new technology. Myra Hess, for example, was terrified of the recording studio. We are all terrified of the red light. But it did not inhibit me. When the red light came on in the recording studio I got down to work and usually only a few takes were necessary.

But the loss of individuality in music-making did sadden me. When I went to see Sir Clifford Curzon in his beautiful house in Highgate, on the edge of Hampstead Heath, he said to me: 'Moura, there was a time when you could listen to the Third Programme and know immediately after a few bars who was playing. If it was Moiseiwitsch, I would say: "That's Benno." That's not possible now.'

I had to agree with him. One of the features that made music a wonderful and unique experience was passing away, sacrificed to technical perfection.

When I went to stay with Herbert von Karajan and his glamorous model wife Eliette at their heavenly chalet in St Moritz it was winter sports time, and the exhilarating mountain air should have made me happy. But I arrived in a very downcast mood nothing could dispel. I had had a review which had terribly upset me; it complained that I had played more wrong notes than I should have.

Karajan was such a dear man. He was the most exciting man too, taking enormous risks, flying his own jet all over the world, benefiting his fellow-artists by persuading the hard-headed Japanese businessmen who ran Sony to set up Sony Classics in Austria.

On my arrival, Eliette was nowhere to be seen. She was a gifted artist and was immured in her studio, painting. Karajan, dressed in a floor-length, vibrantly coloured kaftan, showed me to my room. To Karajan I dared to whinge. Then, alluding to my bad review, I shrugged and said: 'So what! The music is more important.'

Karajan shook his head. 'No, Moura,' he said quietly. 'Today you must play the right notes. People expect it. You can't get away with it any more.' And he quoted a concert-goer who said he preferred Rubinstein's records to his live performance – 'there were fewer wrong notes'.

Karajan was right.

We three took long, healthy walks among the snowy peaks which, together with the superb companionship and excellent food, revived my spirits. I loved our meals together. We would all talk at once, and on one occasion I had the temerity to say to them: 'If one of you would stay silent, I could answer your questions one by one.'

While I was in America I had played at the University of Maryland where an important competition is held annually. In England I sat on the jury of the prestigious Leeds Piano Competition founded by Fanny Waterman. The excitement and drama of these competitions are tremendous. Some people deplore them but I am not one of them. I am all in favour of them because they give young pianists something to work for, and help them build a great deal of necessary endurance and self-confidence. The danger is when executants conclude that there is a difference between playing for an audience and playing for a jury. I don't think there is any difference between the two. Artistes should never believe 'audiences don't know'. Of course I have attended competitions where I disagreed with the verdicts, but this is part of life.

There are so many facets to the issue of temperament. Some younger pianists today, perhaps in their zeal to become total musicians, unwisely try to deny some of their natural tendencies. There was a young German pianist who had been extraordinarily successful in the United States playing Beethoven, but when I heard him play in the finals of the Queen Elisabeth Competition in Brussels, a competition in which as I noted earlier I myself had won the second prize when I was twenty-one, he misguidedly selected the Rachmaninov Second Piano Concerto. I love this concerto and have played it all my life, but I really felt it was all wrong for him physically and emotionally. He did not win and I think he might have done, had he played Beethoven.

The older I grow, the more convinced I am that there are universal truths to all great teaching and great playing. In their writings Gieseking, Neuhaus and Arrau all stress *principles*. People tend to get bogged down in this issue of piano tone being instantaneous, and therefore conclude that what you do after tone is achieved makes no difference. This is true for the tone you have just sounded, but the point is that the condition of your hand and arm makes all the difference for the *next* note you sound.

The ideas of Uncle Tobs had *universal* relevance and I was so delighted to find his ideas increasingly admired, respected and followed in America, where a Matthay Foundation was created.

One of the happinesses of my life in London was that my nephew Christopher Johnstone was near me. He had won a scholarship to an American University where he had studied the history of art and, having graduated, he was now working at the Tate Gallery. His ambition at this time was to research and write a book about the mid-nineteenth-century romantic painter of biblical scenes, John Martin, which he did. It was published with great success in 1974. His father, my brother Tony, had moved to the United States, where he remarried and fathered three more sons, all charming boys.

In London I met heaps of new people as well as renewing old friendships. I enjoyed my career, travelling and hopping on and off aircraft as if they were buses going along Piccadilly. I was described as 'bouncy, chirrupy, cheerful, and completely feminine'.

One day I was strolling down Bond Street when I heard music, good music. I was stopped in my tracks by it and saw a young couple playing their instruments outside Fenwicks. 'You play very well!' I exclaimed, and they smiled.

'We are trained musicians,' they told me, 'and we wanted to come to London to get married here, but we have no money.' They were French. 'We studied at the Conservatoire,' they added, 'but we have been unable to get a job.'

I gave them some money. Moreover, so impressed was I by this talented man and girl that I also gave them the name and telephone number of someone who might be able to help them get work. Later, when I played at Newcastle upon Tyne, one of the orchestra came up to me after the concert. It was the girl I had seen in Bond Street, the bride. 'Remember me?' she asked, smiling. 'We're married now, and we are both working – thanks to that introduction you gave us.'

At a dinner-party given by Lord and Lady Erroll of Hale I met a most interesting and attractive man, Edward Heath. We were exact contemporaries and found we had a great deal in common. He was and is one of the most musically conscious people I know. He was not an easy man to talk to, but I am a great talker and I made up for both of us. He had a deep love, even a passion, for music, having won an organ scholarship to Balliol College, Oxford. This English church tradition in music, somewhat austere, had almost completely passed me by. It could be said that I had hardly been aware of it in my career. Ted Heath had an excellent mind, complete integrity, and no small talk. He was a serious, ambitious politician.

When Ted and I met we were both unattached and the press quickly seized on our friendship as gossip fodder. Ted was a bachelor but he liked women, and although he was shy, when his love of music or the sea broke down his shyness, he became affable. 'Music takes the chill off public life,' he explained.

My most cherished London friends were Reresby and Penelope Sitwell. Penelope is an excellent amateur pianist who studied in Paris, and I was invited to stay at Renishaw, the Derbyshire mansion, to play for a charity function she was organizing to reopen the ballroom at Renishaw, closed for many years. Renishaw is a beautiful and graceful house with wonderful associations. William Walton composed *Façade* to Edith Sitwell's poems while Sacheverell Sitwell, Reresby's father, wrote a superb biography of Liszt. One of my most treasured possessions is a copy of this book, inscribed to me by the author. I was very sensitive to the romantic and artistic history of Renishaw; its atmosphere was alive with the imagination of poets and artists of great sensibility and genius. Over the chimney-piece in the dining-room hung a portrait of a boy wearing a pink satin suit who is said to haunt Renishaw.

After I had finished playing I decided to go to bed early so that I should be up in good time for my journey to Chequers the following day. Ted Heath had invited me to the first party of his premiership in 1970 and I could not possibly miss that. In the large, rambling house I got rather muddled in the various corridors and lost my way to my room. Finally I met a fellow-guest who seemed to know his way about the house and kindly escorted me to my room. On the way we talked of ghosts. As I undressed for bed I thought over our conversation and wondered if indeed it was true that Renishaw had a ghost, or ghosts.

I went to sleep at once in the huge four-poster bed and I dreamed vividly. In my dream I was married to a passionate

Italian and I awoke about three o'clock with the distinct sensation that I was being ardently kissed on the mouth. It was so real. I went to the bathroom for a cooling drink of water, put out the light again and then I heard an extraordinary hissing sound emanating from the fireplace, followed by bangs such as one hears in Paris theatres before the play begins. I put my head under the bedclothes in terror and fell asleep.

The next thing I knew was the housekeeper waking me up. She had brought me my breakfast tray. 'Did you sleep well?' she asked. I told her about my dream and the strange noises and she nearly dropped the tray in my lap. Then Reresby, wearing a dressing-gown, came in, smiling. 'Tell me everything!' he demanded. 'We have a ghost who kisses the girls.'

'Why should he kiss me?' I asked.

'It's the boy in pink. He's thanking you for reopening the ballroom.'

I went to Chequers several times and sometimes I was asked to play the piano for Ted Heath's guests. Ted has described himself as a romantic. He was and is a perfect host. He hosted a party of twelve friends to Glyndebourne, ordering a perfect dinner and excellent wine in advance. At Covent Garden, when his other guests refused drinks in the interval, Ted went to the bar and ordered champagne. 'I know Moura likes champagne,' he explained. On another occasion, after a charity concert for which I had worn a black chiffon gown, he asked critically: 'Why did you wear that colour?'

'I felt it was suitable for a classical pianist,' I replied. 'What would you have said if I had worn a bright lime-green dress?'

'I would just say that you looked very charming, Moura,' he said. 'Don't wear black again.'

Ted was also a religious man, and although he did not talk about it, had served an interesting period as news editor of the *Church Times* – 'a political fish in holy water,' as he has described this period of his life.

But when the press began to write about us in a more suggestive way Ted was embarrassed, unhappy and anxious. It was all nonsense of course to hint, as one or two newspapers did, that we might be about to marry. We were just the proverbial good friends. I rebuked him once, when he had been fishing, because he had not given me any of the cod he had caught.

'Of course not,' he replied. 'I know you only eat caviare!'

# 8

# Healing Hands

I had lost a great deal of the *joie de vivre* which has always been part of my nature. I had an anxiety neurosis, and I did not always play as well as I expected myself to do.

My bedroom was on the top floor of 44 Bruton Place, a large room with en suite bathroom and dressing-room, lined with mirrored cupboards which held all the long gowns that are a necessary part of the equipment of a modern woman concert pianist. They were like a scintillating rainbow when the doors were opened.

One night in December, while stretching like a cat in the night, I thought I felt a lump in my right breast. I put my hand on it. Surely I had imagined it? But I had not. There was definitely something there. I could not believe it. I, who had always been so strong. This could not be happening to me. I passed a terrible night of waiting for the morning to come, and then at the earliest possible moment I telephoned my doctor. 'Come over right away,' he instructed.

He examined it. 'I'm afraid it is,' he told me tersely. 'I will send you for another examination by a surgeon.' A room was immediately reserved for me at a hospital.

I went home to Bruton Place in a daze. And then the full horror of it all suddenly struck me. My mind raced about in all directions, searching for escape. Should I consult a healer? I believed in such people and their powers. Or surely some new wonder drug had been been perfected? Science and medicine have achieved such marvellous cures, and I was after all the granddaughter and great-granddaughter of physicians and surgeons, men with healing hands.

I seized the telephone and dialled a friend in New York. 'Marion,' I asked urgently, 'didn't you have an operation years ago?'

'Why are you asking me this?' she demanded.

I told her and she responded with instinctive generosity.

'Come to New York. Now. Fly over and we will pay for everything. We will have another opinion.'

I cancelled the hospital bed and rang BOAC at once. There were no vacant seats and the receptionist's cool voice reminded me that it was late December, only two days to Christmas Day. They would put my name on a waiting-list in case there should be a cancellation. I stressed the urgency. Were all my papers in order? I rummaged among all my files and found my passport. But, to my dismay, the vaccination certificate, without which BOAC would not allow me on the plane, had expired. Fate decreed I should have to stay in London. I tried to telephone my doctor, but it was Christmas and he had already gone to the country for a well-earned rest with his family. None of my family was near me. I was alone with my fear and foreboding.

Then I remembered a friend with whom I had always felt a sympathy, a doctor whom I had last met in New York: Brian Warren (now Sir Brian Warren). I quickly found his London number, dialled it and, with hope and dread, heard the ringing tone. Was he there? Would he listen? Was what I was doing unethical? Whether it was or not, Brian was at home and he listened to what I told him with all the understanding I expected and longed for.

He came at once to Bruton Place, bundled me into his car and drove me to the King Edward VII Hospital for Officers, also known as 'Sister Agnes', to which he was professionally attached. Richard Handley, the surgeon, examined me and booked me in for the day after Boxing Day. My father, brothers, uncles and my first husband had all been officers in the British armed forces so I was to be welcomed as an in-patient. I was to arrive at 5 p.m.

The 24th, 25th and 26th of December had still to be got through. My mantelshelf was heaped with invitations and I decided to go to all the parties. Why not? What had I to lose? What was the point of staying at home, fretting about what was to happen to me? I told just one woman friend and she at once offered to drive me to the hospital on the 27th. So off I went, dressed as gaily as I knew how, to the Christmas parties and thoroughly enjoyed them – the laughter, the gossip, the champagne, the food. At night, however, on my return to Bruton Place, it was a different story. I could not sleep, or only fitfully. The second my head touched the pillow my imagination was switched on, and I could see only too clearly in my mind's eye visions of myself on the operating-table.

At last the 27th arrived. It was sunless. I packed my prettiest nightgowns and negligées. I also packed my tapestry, a bag of brightly coloured wools, books, radio, writing-paper and envelopes.

It was dark, of course, when my faithful friend came for me shortly after four o'clock. She was smiling brightly, although the expression in her eyes radiated sympathy and concern. We drove in silence through the West End streets brilliant with Christmas lights, the shop windows crowded with tinselled toys and all the trifles associated with Christmas.

At the hospital, in my comfortable, warm room, the nurse told me to undress and get into bed. Supper would be brought to me. I could watch television. Nothing would happen to me until the following morning.

I changed into a nightgown, got into bed, closed my eyes and tried to relax. I felt tired. I had lain there less than half an hour when I heard a quiet knock at the door. 'Come in,' I called.

An elderly priest came into the room. He told me he had retired but had been recruited as a hospital chaplain. It had been a long time since I had had any conversation with a priest, other than Father Charles-Roux at social occasions. I had not been to Mass or Confession for some years. He stood by the side of my bed.

'Father,' I began. It was extraordinarily easy and simple and comforting to address this strange priest thus: 'Father'. I felt at that moment like a child, trusting, putting myself and my life in the healing hands of others. I told him I had twice married, outside the Church, and twice divorced, but that I had never lost my Catholic faith.

'When did you last go to Confession?' he inquired.

I could not remember. 'Some years ago,' I replied.

'Then I suggest you do so now.' he said. 'Right away.'

So I did, there and then, confess to him, as briefly as I could. Father gave me absolution.

'Will you start going to Mass again, starting next Sunday?'

'Yes, I will, Father,' I said.

'Will you promise?'

'I promise.'

And that night I slept peacefully, like a baby.

The next day was the 28th. But the ordeal I was to go through did not occur in the morning as I hoped. I passed the day in a miasma of apprehension and it was not until five o'clock that I was admitted to the operating theatre. There was to be a biopsy.

When I woke up I was in bed in my room, feeling very shivery. I heard Dick Handley speaking, perhaps not realizing I was awake but still under sedation. I understood at once what had happened to me. I took the news calmly. 'I'm cold,' I told the night nurse. 'Could I have some more blankets?' I drifted off to sleep, still under the anaesthetic.

The next day I woke up to a room filled with flowers. I sat up and breathed in the lovely, refreshing fragrance, the colours gladdened my eyes, and realized the whole world must know now. My friend and agent for many years, Emmie Tillett, of the strong personality and with a rare understanding of musicians, was the one person I had told, and she had told everybody else. I sat up and, feeling better already, reached for my tapestry.

But I could not move my left arm. Or, whenever I did, I almost screamed with pain. I never listened to the radio at home; it seemed as if I never had the time. So I switched it on and heard some most interesting programmes I had never dreamed existed. And I found I could manage to hold the canvas in my left hand and work the wools with my right.

Sisters, doctors and all the staff were kindness itself. Matron made a special point of seeing the New Year in with me, and we toasted each other and the wonderful hospital that was taking such marvellous care of me, in champagne.

I did not have to have chemotherapy; I was to try and move my hand and arm a little more every day. But I did not dare do so for fear of the excruciating pain it caused. I was taught to stand up against a wall, rest my hand on it, and each day try to move my hand upwards a little, maybe only a fraction of an inch.

Ten days passed serenely. At about six in the evening friends and colleagues trooped in bearing champagne and whisky and we had wonderful parties round my bed. Lorraine, a sweet young woman friend, came nearly every day to do my hair and make me up, and chose a pretty housecoat for me to wear for my sallies down the hospital corridor.

Exercising my considerable will-power, I had managed so far to ignore completely the loss I had suffered. I would not let myself think or brood about it. One day only did I let my mind wander back to what had happened. The dreadful realization dawned on me and I wept helplessly and bitterly. I called a nurse and sobbed to her that I could not stop weeping. 'Take a good slug of Scotch,' she counselled cheerfully. 'And when you've drunk it, take another!'

Excellent advice. I felt better, got out my tapestry charts and decided to start the most difficult of all the designs. *That* would keep my mind fully occupied, I reasoned sternly to myself. Crying was useless.

Along the corridor was 'the Nursery', a ward of five beds occupied by men, from a twenty-nine-year-old to one in his seventies. One day one of the nurses had difficulty opening a bottle of champagne for me. 'I'll ask one of the men in the Nursery to do it,' she said.

'Who is it for?' the men asked her curiously.

'The lady in Room 23,' she replied.

'Tell her to come and drink it with us,' they quipped.

Quickly and deftly one of the men untwisted the wire and began pushing the cork out of the bottle. I could hear the 'pop' in my room. The nurse returned and relayed the invitation.

'Let's go!' I said eagerly, while Lorraine, who was with me, found and helped me into my prettiest housecoat.

We had a great party. No one asked my name, nor why I was in the hospital, but they invited me to come to see them again the next evening. By then they knew I was a pianist and clamoured for me to play for them.

'But there's no piano!' I protested. I could not have played anyway at that stage of my convalescence. I could still hardly move my left hand from my side. However, I promised I would bring in my record-player and some records and choose a short recital for them to listen to. They were delighted, and a time was fixed when there would be no hospital trolleys coming round making a clatter.

I telephoned EMI and Decca the next day and asked them to send round some recordings of mine, and the following evening all was ready for our informal concert. The five men and I gathered round the record-player, each with a drink in his hand or by his bed, listening to one after another recital I had recorded several years ago. From time to time a doctor or nurse would pop in to examine a patient, but sensing the complete absorption in the music, would slink out again silently. An hour was spent listening intently, and then I left the men to go back to my room for my supper.

'Please come again tomorrow evening!' they called out to me.

So for three nights running I selected the records and gave a little concert. It was fun for me too, to have their company, and it gave me a chance to learn all about them. The twenty-nine-year-old was a white hunter from Kenya who had been out on safari with his brother, had taken aim with his rifle at a rhinoceros and the bullet had ricocheted off the animal's horn and killed his brother. As soon as he was allowed to walk, he would come and sit with me in my room while I did my tapestry and talk to me. This was excellent therapy for me, the very best remedy God could bestow.

After the most restful three weeks of my life I returned home to Bruton Place, got down on my knees and thanked God for letting me live. And then I thanked God for leaving me my hands. I promised him that from that day onwards I would work harder than at any time in my life. God had given me this gift, this divine gift of music, which I felt I had not sufficiently appreciated. I had taken it for granted, and spent my life loving and fretting and pursuing the transient happiness of the love of men, rather than concentrating on my music.

I practised regularly every day, but I had no strength. I began to cry, to feel sorry for myself. I wailed to friends that I was finished as a concert pianist and that I would never play in public again. My surgeon, Dick Handley, had told me that it would be three months before I would be able to give my first recital. Emmie Tillett, knowing my enthusiasm and resilience, said she was sure I could do it in two months' time. She meant to be encouraging, and I was keen and tried even harder. As with everything else in my life, I was far too vehement.

Brian Warren chided me. 'You have been overdoing things,' he said. 'You will not play before three months,' adding: 'You must go away for a complete rest.'

I went to the South of France for ten days and returned a new woman.

I have described the emotional effect on me of this operation, but the financial aspect was calamitous. I was a working woman who for three months had earned nothing at all. I had had to cancel all my concerts and my overdraft was enormous, demanding drastic action.

Emmie Tillett came to lunch and we discussed the future. 'Should I go and live in a one-room studio?' I asked her.

'Give it a year, Moura,' she replied calmly. 'And then we'll decide.'

Brian Warren, too, was against my leaving Bruton Place just then, pointing out that two traumatic experiences, one after the other, the operation and then a house move, would be more than I could stand. I should be risking a severe breakdown. And he reminded me that I had made a wonderful recovery.

Three months to the day after the operation, I played at the Royal Festival Hall, Prokofiev's Piano Concerto No. 4 Op. 53 for the left hand. I sent tickets to Dick Handley, who was appalled that I was playing this formidable work. It was the left side of my body on which he had operated.

But I was not satisfied with my performances. I needed help – badly. The reviews were not as good as I should have liked them to be. I was particularly upset to read some derogatory comments about some Debussy Préludes which critics of my earlier performances had described as 'magical'. One can never afford to play at less than one's best, regardless of the occasion or the audience. Concert-goers are extremely discriminating and respond almost at once to differences in the quality of the concerts. I was in danger of losing my self-confidence entirely.

One of the pieces of advice that I most treasure from Uncle Tobs was his insistence that pianists should play works for which they are physically and temperamentally suited. And he also used to say: 'Moura, when in Rome, do as the Romans do.' The virtuosity of works like the Rachmaninov concerti and preludes felt natural and easy to me. Uncle Tobs taught me not to resist the inclination to be a virtuoso player.

The automatic 'type-casting' which prevails in the concert world is rather like the stereotyping of actors in Hollywood. 'We have no Rachmaninov for her,' replied one concert manager to an inquiry as to why I was not engaged for a particular series of concerts.

The operation had come at the right moment. It brought me to my senses and gave me a new sense of values. And it made me absolutely determined to go back and find out where I had gone wrong musically.

Ilona Kabos was a Hungarian pianist who had been married to the pianist Louis Kentner. She taught at the Juilliard School in New York, where she was almost worshipped by her students. She had a fantastic ear, was a very severe critic, speaking in short, curt sentences, and utterly, even brutally, honest. She was now in her seventies but she dressed in an extraordinary way, girlish, even coquettish, at odds with her austere attitude to musical performance. She had given up performing altogether, for she had discovered a truly remarkable gift for teaching. Practically everyone one knew had, at some time or another, gone to play for her and seek her sage counsel, musical or personal. Joan Moore (the Countess of Drogheda) was another who consulted her. John Ogdon, before competing at Moscow, flew back to London to play to Ilona, before returning to Moscow for the final, and to win the competition.

As I sat in the hall of Ilona's house, waiting for her to be free, Gina Bachauer emerged. We talked and Gina told me that whenever she had a big engagement, in London or New York, she always played for Ilona first.

I begged Ilona to tell me everything I did wrong, and she did. 'What's this?' she asked. 'Where is the famous Lympany technique?'

Ilona did not destroy my confidence, as the newspaper critics had when I read their condemnations in print, which was so public. With Ilona the sessions were more like consultations with a psychiatrist. She became a trusted friend and mentor, just what I needed at this time. I found that I spent half my lessons confiding all sorts of things to her and relying upon her opinion and judgement completely. 'You'll find you'll get that technique back again,' she said. And, looking critically at my hair one day, 'What *do* you think you have done?' she barked at me. 'A pianist wears a bun, that's all,' she added.

I was put in my place like a schoolgirl. Her attitude was the traditional one that a woman musician eschews any attempt at glamour, elegance, chic, and espouses a pure, reserved and restrained look and life-style. That would not be true to myself; I have never been like that and find it false to assume it – depressing and unnecessary. A critic has described me as 'enigmatic' and 'un-English'. Perhaps it is the reverse of puritanical: Catholic and continental.

'Do you *have* to go to every party you are invited to?' Ilona demanded on another occasion.

I explained that I lived alone, worked all day alone at the piano and it did me good to go out in the evenings, to meet and talk to all sorts of people. She was pitiless and disapproving, but continued to teach me where and how I was going wrong. She could tell if I was faking a passage I did not know too well technically, or any emotion I did not really feel. But she never destroyed me or my individuality. That was her great strength.

Ted Heath was sceptical. 'What can you teach Moura?' he asked her.

Playing in a concert hall is a very different matter from playing in a drawing-room. The softest sound must be heard at the very back of the auditorium.

'I bring out what is in her,' Ilona told Ted Heath. 'I teach her to project it.' It was true. She did that – and much more.

'Play with your wrists low, as if you were playing inside the keys,' she would say to me. 'That's the only way you will make your pianissimos sound.'

Ilona also made me work longer than I had ever worked before. 'Go to the piano at ten o'clock in the morning and stay there till one o'clock, and then you can certainly manage another two or three hours in the afternoon,' she told me.

I protested that that was too much; I had never practised more than four hours a day and I was already overtired. But Ilona was implacable. She wanted every note perfect. It is expected today. 'Sit up straight,' she barked at me. 'Don't throw yourself around so much!' I felt like a wilful child. 'You can play those works standing on your head.' I worked, trying to do as she told me. 'Practise slowly,' she ordered, 'as if you had all the time in the world. Never practise in a panic.'

We had very much the same temperament; we were both reckless spendthrifts. Her brusque manner never upset me because it cloaked the gentlest and most generous heart and spirit.

'Emotion comes from the bottom of one's stomach!' Ilona declared one day to my amusement.

She was right. When one breathed deeply, a sigh, with emotion, with sadness, with passion, while playing, it was there at the bottom of the stomach that one felt it. Ralph Kirkpatrick wrote that rhythm is felt in the solar plexus. All the martial arts of Japan are directed from the lower stomach. The stomach 'carries' the body. Then I remembered what the greatest woman pianist of her day, Youra Guller, had once said to me: 'If you want to create atmosphere, sit absolutely still at the piano!' I had been young and untried then. 'If you do not move, the audience will not dare to either, and there will be utter stillness, and your mood will get through.'

Ilona decided that I should give a recital at the Queen Elizabeth Hall. I have never been good at making programmes; I used to put into my programme whatever pieces I wanted to play. Ilona and I planned it together: the Haydn E Minor Sonata, the Schumann F Sharp Minor Sonata and, in the second half of the programme, the twenty-four Preludes by Chopin. It was a really beautiful programme and luckily I was able to play it at about seven concerts before the London recital so I was really quite confident.

Since my operation, out of gratitude for the marvellous surgery and treatment I had received, I felt I must add my efforts to those of others, and help raise funds for further research. I had given a recital at St James's Palace in the presence of the Duchess of Kent. Now, six months later, I was to give another recital for the same charity in the country, in a newly converted barn. Most of the men who had worked on the building were to be present, and I was resolved to put all I had learned, relearned and was still learning from Ilona into the performance.

The programme included the Chopin B Minor Sonata. Afterwards the foreman confessed to the owner of the barn: 'I've never cried in my life, except when my mother died, but I cried tonight when Moura Lympany played the slow movement of the sonata.'

A member of the committee, who had attended the recital at St James's Palace, asked me: 'What has happened to your playing? You are so much more relaxed. You seem another person.'

An old fellow-student from RAM days who had also studied with Coviello, came to hear me play at a recital. She had spent a joyful life as a teacher and accompanist. She later wrote to me most movingly:

> I have watched your wonderful career with such pride, I couldn't have conveyed to you what your playing meant to me. I was so grateful that you told me you had had cancer, because I think this explains an even further, deeper dimension in your playing since I last heard you some years ago. Your command of the keyboard has always been phenomenal, but you have an emotional and spiritual depth which quite bowled me over.

And when I was asked to play the Haydn Piano Concerto in D Major and to conduct from the piano the newly formed Cambridge Symphony Orchestra at their inaugural concert at St John's, Smith Square, it was a challenge I could not resist. Later I played with them at Great Yarmouth in Norfolk. Jonathan Wearn, their artistic director, wrote to me, saying:

> . . . This is to formally record our thanks from the Orchestra and the people of Cambridge for what became for us under your leadership an inspiring musical experience.
>
> It was interesting for us in the early hours of the morning to run tapes of other pianists and yourself in the Haydn D Major. . . .
>
> . . . Your performance, musically speaking, is way beyond the aspirations of 'a good performance'. It is great music from one of the most important musical musicians of our time.

Artists rarely cancel concerts, for, apart from the resultant ill-will, no performance, no pay. Some artists will not deputize for others, but I have never minded doing so.

One day I was telephoned and asked if I could leave for Yugoslavia to play three concerts. It was at the time of the Greek Revolution and the King of Greece had flown out of the country to exile. I was to deputize for the Greek pianist Gina Bachauer, who not only was devoted to the King and Queen but had family and owned property in Greece. She was prostrate and unable to fulfil her engagements in Yugoslavia.

'When do I have to leave?' I asked.

'In an hour,' I was told.

I pushed two evening gowns into a suitcase with other necessities and was ready.

In the car en route to the airport I was given instructions. I was to play the Tchaikovsky and Brahms B Flat Concerto, neither of which I had played for at least a year, in Belgrade, before going on to Zagreb for a third concert.

On the plane I studied the music and the next morning in Belgrade managed to get some practice in before the rehearsal. The concerts successfully over, the British Ambassador and his wife came round to see me in my dressing-room, to find me in a highly nervous state, just about to leave for the railway station and the night-sleeper to Zagreb. I was supperless and alone, and outside the concert hall a blizzard raged. I could not speak the language. They were deeply concerned at my plight and begged to be allowed to help.

'Could you possibly get me a picnic basket?' I asked. 'I'm hungry.'

They kindly drove me to the station, and meanwhile the Embassy prepared a picnic basket, which arrived in time: we had an hour to wait in the Embassy car in the snow, for the train was late. But I had a gorgeous supper in my sleeper.

Then one day the telephone rang at 12.30. Would I deputize straight away for John Lill at St John's, Smith Square? The concert was being broadcast and I could play what I liked. Luckily I had practised for two hours that morning, although I had been playing bridge the night before till the early hours. I quickly changed into a long dress, rushed out and hailed a passing taxi in Berkeley Square. All the way to Westminster my mind raced over the programme and on arrival I had settled on the Bach Chromatic Fantasy and Fugue, some Debussy and Rachmaninov preludes, and the Chopin Scherzo No. 3 in C Sharp Minor.

Lill was there, looking anxious. One of his fingers was bound up with Elastoplast, after a carbuncle had burst and spilled blood all over the piano keys. He thanked me for taking his place.

I also deputized once for Jean-Philippe Collard, nearly thirty years my junior, when he could not play in Kansas City. I played an all-Chopin recital. Emmie Tillett once said to me: 'Moura, you are my most dependable artist. You have never let me down.'

I used to be able to learn a new piece in two days; if you are playing without the music, you can let yourself go. The more you know a piece, the more you can let yourself go, do things on the spur of the moment. Because at that moment you are feeling this is very sad or this is very jolly, or whatever. But if you are busy reading notes, how can you play with your heart?

When I went to Scotland to play at a charity concert in aid of the National Trust for Scotland, Princess Alexandra was to be present and I was to be given hospitality for the night by the Earl and Countess of Wemyss at Gosford House. The Earl is president of the National Trust for Scotland and lord lieutenant for East Lothian. I packed an evening dress along with my concert gown in case a dinner-party should precede the function.

I travelled all day to Edinburgh, where a car met me to take me on the most beautiful route through the Pentland Hills shrouded with rosy, misty sunshine on one side and the glowering waters of the Firth of Forth on the other. On arrival at the magnificent Adam mansion, I was greeted with such kindly warmth by my hosts and given most welcome tea beside a roaring log fire. Then Lady Wemyss showed me to my room. 'What would you like to do before dinner?' she asked me. 'Would you like a bath?'

'What are you going to do?' I replied.

'I'm going to the kitchen,' said Lady Wemyss.

'May I follow you?'

'Yes, do come.'

So off we went to the mansion's kitchen where I expected to find a cook, maid and butler at the very least, preparing the dinner. But it was deserted. Lady Wemyss took hold of some pots.

'What are you doing?' I asked.

'I'm making the evening meal,' she replied. 'I'm making two dinners at the same time because my daughter is coming in two days. I'll do two chickens and two rices – two of everything – and put one lot in the freezer ready for when she comes.'

'Can I help you?' I offered.

'Would you really like to help?' Lady Wemyss put an apron round me and I began adding raisins to the rice.

Then Lord Wemyss came in. 'What would you like me to do?' he asked his wife.

'Just top up our glasses with wine,' replied the Countess.

When the meal was ready, 'We'll go into the dining-room,' said Lady Wemyss. So I helped her load the trolley and we wheeled it together out of the kitchen. We were all still in our day clothes.

The dining-room looked beautiful: the long table laden with all the family silver and glass, shining and elegant.

'I'll light the candles,' said Lord Wemyss, and the three of us sat down and ate a delicious dinner.

I gave a recital at the Convent of Our Lady at Southam, where my aunt, Sister Mary John, now aged ninety-two, was still active, helping an exiled Polish man with his Shakespeare studies for a forthcoming examination. 'God be praised for the Grand Talent He has entrusted to you,' she wrote to me afterwards. 'I did pray that the Holy Spirit would enlighten you.'

Before my concerts now in the artist's room I thanked God for leaving me my hands. Father Charles-Roux of St Ethelreda's Church, Ely Place, wrote to me: 'Dear Princess Mourosi (musically that is the way you ought to be called) . . . I have heard you twice on Radio 3 once in Franck's Variations and then in some Poulenc. . . . God bless you and give you triumph since "music is peace and the Angels' art". . . . John-Maria Charles-Roux.'

Ilona Kabos helped me on the long climb back and I am only one of many who remember her with love and gratitude.

Ilona was herself already ill with cancer. I missed her more than I can say. She left a terrible, irreplaceable gap in my life and work. Suddenly there was this void; I had lost this great and good friend and teacher, and I had many engagements looming. I was to play Rachmaninov's Third Piano Concerto at the Europalia in Brussels, Antwerp and Namur, and a solo recital in London was to follow, the biggest test for an artist, since the critics come and their reviews are read by everyone.

I scurried round and found three people whose opinions I respected, who were prepared to listen to me play. They all had different comments to make on my performance and by the time of the recital I found I was terribly confused, trying to please three different people, struggling to remember all their criticisms.

That was a hopeless state of affairs. I had the sense to put them out of my mind just in time. When one comes on to the platform, one must forget everything one has been taught and let the music flow from – through – oneself, as if improvising. One should only think of the mood, the line, and forget about the mechanics of the whole thing. Uncle Tobs had a phrase: 'Let it play itself.'

On 6 January 1979, 'The year certainly started nicely for me,' I wrote to a friend in astonishment and pride, 'as I got the CBE in the New Year's Honours List.' My appointment as a Commander of the British Empire coincided with my fiftieth golden jubilee anniversary of my début at the age of twelve as a concert pianist. With my nephew Christopher I went to Buckingham Palace to receive the decoration. I celebrated with a charity concert in aid of Cancer Research on Monday, 4 June. The Prince of Wales graciously consented to be present and I reserved the Royal Festival Hall.

It was a marvellous, heart-warming occasion attended by many many old and new friends and colleagues and family. My brother Tony flew from America; my nephew was present, and so was my darling aunt Sister Mary John. When she was presented to the Prince of Wales, His

Royal Highness talked to her for a long time. A contingent of friends including His Excellency Walter Loridan, who had been Belgian Ambassador in New York, came from Belgium, while after the recital Baron Robert Vaes and Baroness Vaes, the Belgian Ambassador and his wife, hosted a dinner in my honour in the upstairs restaurant at the Royal Festival Hall.

Later that very special year of my golden jubilee as a concert pianist, I was proud to play at a recital for Baron and Baroness Vaes at the Belgian Embassy, graced by the presence of Queen Elizabeth, the Queen Mother. Belgium had played such an important part in my life. I loved the country and the people. It had been home to me. Afterwards, Madame Vaes gave me as a souvenir the letter, written in her own hand by Queen Elizabeth, the Queen Mother, in which Her Majesty alluded to 'the exquisite playing of Moura Lympany'. To my great joy I also received the Décoration de Commandeur de l'Ordre de la Couronne du Royaume de Belgique, in recognition 'des services rendus'.

# 9

# 'God Sent Me to Rasiguères'

*Racines*

C'est au village de Rasiguères
Que j'ai appris à marcher naguère
Comme un enfant heureux
Entre la vigne et le cerisier généreux,
bercé par le chant des cigales
Qui charment l'onde de l'Agly opale
dès que le jour se pare d'un soleil indiscret
pour réveiller la nature et tous ses secrets . . .
accompagnée de moments de tristesse
mais avide de beaucoup de tendresse.
J'entends encore le crépitement du feu que j'attise
sur les chemins ornés de coquelicots où siffle la bise,
car il faut bien des racines, et j'en veux pour moi-même,
persuadé d'être de ceux que l'on aime
pour ne pas avoir oublié dans ma bouche
le souffle de la Tramontane farouche.

Marcel Jourda, 1988

All my life when I have played 'big' works, which need a lot of strength, like the Tchaikovsky, Rachmaninov and Khachaturian concerti, I have tended to put the emotion into my throat, a kind of grunting not heard by the audience, of course, but resulting in a loss of voice after the performance.

My voice was quite croaky at these times, and I was told I sounded very sexy, like Marlene Dietrich or Lauren Bacall. That was flattering, but nevertheless I began to worry about it, especially when I developed a cough I could not get rid of. My throat was constantly irritated and my voice so low, at times I sounded like a man or a contralto with tonsillitis. I went to see a throat specialist who listened patiently while I described my symptoms. I paused for breath.

'You talk too much!' he commented. 'You work too hard, you play too hard.' (He meant I enjoyed myself too much. I burned the candle at both ends.) He advised me to leave London, and to seek a warm, dry climate in the mountain air, and not to talk for a month. He assured me that then my voice would return to normal.

Not talk for a whole month! It was quite a severe sentence, for I love good conversation.

I went back to my house in Bruton Place utterly *bouleversée*. To take his advice was not easy; I had not the slightest idea where to go and my diary was, as usual, full of engagements, social and musical. There were lots of places I could go to where the weather is good most of the time, and where I could stay with congenial friends, but I realized that I could not rest properly if I were a guest. Naturally one has to try and fit in with one's hostess's plans. Whether one stayed at home or went out, one had to talk – exactly what my specialist did not want me to do. I decided I must go somewhere where I could be quite alone. I needed a simple, small nest of my own.

I picked up a book, *A Farmhouse in Provence*, written by a great friend of mine, an American, Mary Roblee Henry. It painted in words a magical picture of rural France. I had always loved France: the Mecca of good food, wine, couture. French had been the language I first learned to speak at the knee of a young French girl whose name I had long forgotten. My schooldays had been spent at a Belgian convent. I felt an allegiance to France, and French culture.

Sunday came and I was no nearer making a decision.

Upstairs on the second floor of my house in Bruton Place was my bedroom, and I lay in bed reading *The Sunday Times*. A small advertisement caught my eye: *Come to the hottest, driest part of France and rent our village home while you look around for somewhere to buy*. The advertisement seemed to be directed straight at me; I was intrigued and sent off for details immediately.

The house was in the Roussillon region of the Pyrénées-Orientales in southern France. The rent was not modest and I was warned that the house was small and primitive. It belonged to an English couple who had bought the house and contents after the death of the owners. Nothing had been done to it. I waved all discouragement aside and, as soon as I could, shut up my house, switched on the Ansafone, instructed that no letters were to be sent on to me, and set off. I had taken the French house for two weeks.

It was June and the plane trees in London were in full young leaf, that piercing green which almost hurts one's eyes. Behind me I left the patio-garden I had made opening out of my kitchen on the first floor, and this was just beginning to show geraniums in flower, as well as begonias and lilies and roses. But the air was cold and damp, and I was perpetually clearing my throat. I knew I was doing the right thing in taking the throat specialist's advice.

For the last part of the journey the train followed a spectacular route beside the sea coast and the salt flats on one side, mountains and lakes on the other, peopled by occasional fishermen, rod and line in hand. I felt the most extraordinary sensation, a real physical thrill, and I knew, as I turned my head constantly from side to side so as not to miss a second of the breathtaking scenery, that I was falling in love with the land there.

On arrival at Perpignan, a town I did not know, I got into a taxi and asked the driver to take me to Rasiguères. Did he know it?

'Oui.' He nodded. 'Un petit village perdu.'

He put the taxi into gear and off we went. I felt very excited.

The village was thirty kilometres north-west of Perpignan. On the drive I looked eagerly about me. We were soon away and surrounded by mountains, the road winding round and round the lower slopes and gradually climbing. The sky was a cloudless cerulean blue and the thrilling landscape carved into a series of terraces on the mountains, patterned into regular rows with the black, gnarled stumps of the pruned vines sprouting vivid green leaves. Here and there great outcrops of red-striated rock loomed up beside the road. Red for the iron-ore the soil contains, hence the name of the region: Roussillon. The nearer one gets to Rasiguères, the more beautiful it is.

We passed through many villages till we came to the small town of Estagel and then to the important landmark village of Latour de France with its massive stone keep dominating the surrounding valley, which once marked the border between France and Catalonia, and to the hamlet of Planèzes. We had been driving for half an hour. And at last the sign Rasiguères came into view, just before we rounded a hairpin bend, where before my eyes appeared a cluster of stone houses randomly roofed with old red tiles, on the side of a hill above a bridge under which coursed the River Agly.

The little house where I was to stay was up a narrow back street, and the interior was dark and gloomy. There was no bathroom. It was primitive, and I am very fond of my creature comforts. I was dismayed. Why on earth, I asked myself, had I left my lovely house in Mayfair for this?

'Is there a hotel?' I asked Madame Marco, who held the key.

'No,' she replied.

'Is there a restaurant?'

'No.'

'Is there a taxi?'

'No.'

So I realized I should have to stay till the next day.

That first night I went to bed in the little bedroom of the tiny rented house, lonely and lost and uncomfortable after a brief wash in the old stone sink in the downstairs room which doubled as a kitchen and sitting-room, and two aspirins washed down with duty-free whisky for my supper.

The next morning I was woken by sunbeams penetrating the chinks in the window-shutters, and when I rose to open them the sun streamed in, warm and healing to my spirit, and my body, exhausted from the long journey. I looked out at the red roofs and the beautiful old stone, and beyond to the vines all growing lustily in serried, undulating ranks against the dun mountain slopes. Here and there pear trees and apricots and almonds had showered their petals over the earth and their fruits were showing strong. I quickly dressed and went out, found a little *épicerie* open for an hour, bought provisions, and explored further.

I revelled in the scenery and the air and walked for miles among the hills fragrant with thyme, fennel, rosemary and lavender, down to the ravine. Not a house was to be seen anywhere in the strange stillness of the air. I heard a hoopoe (*Upupa epops*) call and recognized a golden oriole (*Oriolus oriolus*.) The clear-running River Agly, whose waters tumbling over the rocks made such lovely music to my town-dweller's ears, came from a source within the mountains, the Gorges de Cucugnan, where eagles nest. The word 'Agly' derives from *aigle*, meaning eagle. To reach the river one had to walk behind the large modern building, the Cave Cooperative. Here in the autumn the vine-growers brought their harvest of grapes to be processed and bottled into wine.

I am not a good swimmer so I was delighted to find that the river water, when I gingerly stepped over the rocks behind the Cave, did not come higher than my head, so I could bathe with confidence. The river-bed was littered with boulders of rose-coloured marble. A flash of iridescent blue among the grey willow leaves signalled a kingfisher. The Agly was bordered with tall bamboo groves so there was complete privacy too, and the water was clear, clean and cool. One could fish; the villagers fished at night for eels. When one strolled out at night, from the interstices of the stone walls gleamed a myriad glow-worms. And nightingales sang.

The danger was that one would sunbathe too much. The villagers begged me not to go out of doors from the hours of twelve to four, when the sun was at its height and the temperature soared into the hundreds. Sunstroke was common among the occasional tourists.

Then there was a rare shower, and the freshening of the air was miraculous. Afterwards, the whole population of the village emerged from the shadowed, shuttered silence of their little houses into the streets, breathing deeply the cooled air, as if in communal thanksgiving for the benison of rain.

All round me were ancient houses with walls several feet thick. A few cats and dogs roamed the streets, and sometimes even slunk through the large drainpipes which lined them. An old church sat in the middle, and a square tower dominated the surrounding houses, all that remained of the ancient château of the powerful Guise family, who had been the seigneurs there before the Revolution. Once a day, four days a week, a bus left the village at 6.30 a.m. for the town of Estagel, ten kilometres away. All round me were the accents of the Midi, French spoken with a Spanish accent, or rather Catalan. Everybody greets everybody else in a village: 'Bonjour Madame', 'Bonjour Monsieur'. The village was full of people.

The first morning I met a man in the vineyards. 'What are you doing here?' he inquired.

'I've had a throat infection,' I said.

'I have had a lung removed,' he responded. 'This is my first visit here in five years.'

'I heard there was a vineyard for sale and I thought I would go and look at it,' I told him.

'Come with me,' said the man, a Monsieur Marcel Galangau, and he took me to a small area where the vines were well advanced in growth. 'If you buy it,' he told me, 'I will sell you my land which is next to it.' It is a courtesy that people always give first refusal to their neighbours.

He pointed out the twenty-five almond trees on his land that he had planted five years earlier. Now they were well grown, the flowers had set and the young almonds promised a bumper crop. I, a stranger, happening to pass through his village looking for a vineyard, and he on his first visit for five years. I told him God had brought us together, but he replied that he did not believe in God. This was surprising, for France is a Catholic country and throughout my many vicissitudes I have always remained staunchly Catholic. But I respect other people's philosophies and shrugged. 'Well,' I told Monsieur Galangau, 'let's call it fate!'

'You must come and meet my wife,' he said, and so I got into his car and he drove me to a handsome modern villa in the middle of the village, almost opposite the Cave, with a pretty, covered veranda in front and steps up to the front door. One of the neighbours alerted Madame Galangau: 'Your husband's got a pretty woman in the car!'

Hélène Galangau was most welcoming and we got on splendidly. She sent for her daughter Marcelle and son-in-law Etienne Dornon. We were soon great friends. I absolutely fell in love with the village and its inhabitants.

I told my new friends Marcel and Hélène Galangau that I would very much like to buy a small property, even if it had only one room with a tiny garden.

'I think I might have something you might like,' he told me.

'Can we go and see it?' I asked.

He got the key.

'I'll come too,' said his daughter Marcelle.

It was a little stone building with a corrugated-iron lean-to hidden away on the other side of the village. Fifty years ago, sheep had been kept there. I eagerly went with him, up the Rue du Centre, round the corner of the *épicerie,* kept by Robert and Josette, then, tucked away in a corner, approached by a narrow path, was La Bergerie, the sheep-fold. There were two entrances, one for the baby lambs and another for the ewes. Through one door I saw a little room with an earthen floor and a wooden ladder in the corner which led up to the loft, and through the other door I saw another room with a fire-hood and a large hand-hewn stone sink. A window over it looked out on to a pocket handkerchief patch of ground, rank with tall weeds and littered with debris, but in the middle was a pear tree. As Monsieur Galangau had used the sheep-fold for the grape-pickers, it had running water and electricity.

'I'll return to London', I told Monsieur Galangau, 'and bring back the money to buy it.'

'Would you like to sign for it?' he asked.

'I can't,' I said. 'I haven't any money.'

'We will go to the Mayor and say we have agreed,' he told me. 'We are willing to sell and you are willing to buy.'

To the *mairie* we went and signed a *promis de vente* then and there. I was asked for a deposit. I rummaged in my bag. 'I've got 500 francs,' I said (about £50).

'That's fine,' said Monsieur Galangau. 'Here's the key.'

I could hardly wait to talk the whole visit over with my decorator friend Martyn Thomas, who was as excited as I was at the prospect of converting the sheep-fold into a holiday retreat. Would there be enough room for a baby grand piano? There must be, I declared. As soon as we could arrange it, Martyn and I set off in the Mercedes, my bed tied on the roof-rack, for the long drive across France to take possession of my sheep-fold, La Bergerie, in Rasiguères.

The villagers had said they didn't know winters in Rasiguères, but when we arrived in January it was bitterly cold and snow was falling for the first time for seven years. La Bergerie was unheated, and as we carried the things in from the car we wondered how we would survive.

'Ply me with vino,' ordered Martyn. 'I'll see to it all.'

'I'll sleep upstairs,' I said. 'And you sleep downstairs.'

'Do you think', said Martyn vehemently, 'I'm going to sleep downstairs? Have you seen the hole in the front door?'

I said to myself: 'You never know in life what's going to happen to you!'

Then Martyn asked: 'Have you anything left?'

'Six yards of yellow silk chiffon I was going to make a dress with.'

'I'll have that!' Later, he said: 'Come upstairs. Everything is ready.'

I went upstairs. Two mattresses lay on the floor, two candlesticks at the head of each bed, and over them was a draped canopy of yellow silk chiffon. Gentle white flakes descended. 'D'you see all the holes in the roof?' asked Martyn. It was snowing.

So we went to bed, Martyn fully dressed under his mink coat, and I fully dressed under mine. Luckily we had brought blankets.

The next morning we drove out to buy heaters. Thank God for electricity!

Martyn was in his element planning and designing the interior and exterior of La Bergerie. He spoke French and instructed the builders and plumbers and electricians and carpenters. We were blissfully happy and creative. Martyn, my 'mate,' my *copain*, had an instinctive knowledge of what I would like and what would suit me. As in Bruton Place, he created an interior setting for me that was exuberantly flowery, all the colours brilliant and even clashing, and yet, when put together by him, the effect was magically pretty and gay. Upstairs, a small bathroom had been contrived somehow off the bedroom. And then my furniture was sent out from London.

I was particularly keen to create a garden, as I wanted to eat out, sleep out – that is, rest in my hammock slung from the pear tree in the garden, my greatest relaxation and therapy, in the cool of the evening, listening to the nightingales. My so-called garden consisted of a patch, twenty by thirty feet, of weeds and rubbish with a pear tree in the centre. That was the view from my kitchen window. On two sides there were stone walls and the end of the garden was fenced in by barbed wire.

My first visit as owner lasted only fifteen days, but I went straight to one of the nurseries in Perpignan for some 'instant gardening'. I bought a cherry tree, two peaches and an apricot espalier, a blue hibiscus, three oleanders in different colours, a tamarisk, a *Lagerstroemia*, a *Caesalpinia* and a few rose-bushes. My neighbours, the local grocers Josette and Robert, helped me to put them in. On my next visit Robert told me he had watered my garden every evening. I said: 'How kind of you. Thank you.' He replied that it was only natural, since I was his neighbour.

On my third visit, Martyn, also a keen gardener, came with me. We filled the car with things for the house and plants for the garden – out of my own London patio and from nurseries. So *Rosa filipas* and *Rosa gigantea* were put in, one to cover the stone wall on the right and the other to climb on to and hide the corrugated-iron roof of the kitchen lean-to. At the side of the house I put in a white *Clematis montana* that just took off and started covering the other side of the roof. People came from all sides of the village to admire 'the million stars' of a plant hitherto unknown to them.

I planted the climbing rose Parade on one side of the pear tree and Garland on the other. Everybody commiserated with me, predicting that there would be no pears with all those roses strangling them. However, when the pear blossom and the Garland roses were out together, they all came again to admire and stood in wonder, saying it looked as if snow had covered the tree. Both roses grew rapidly, but despite their reaching to the top of the tree and cascading down, I still had an excellent crop of golden pears.

On the stone wall on the right we planted Mermaid, Claude Monet's favourite single rose – I so love those honey-coloured saucer blooms with toothbrush stamens; then a yellow Banksian rose, and *Jasminum nudiflorum*. We also planted a magnolia, a forsythia, a camellia and some fuchsias from my London pots.

To the left of the house a little path led to the garden, and here against the stone wall of the house I planted Albertine, Altissima, Galway Bay, and Pink Perpetué, hoping that they too would climb on to the corrugated-iron roof of the lean-to kitchen. Each year they just stopped short. I never found out whether the winds – the famous tramontane – blowing hot from the mountains were the cause, or whether my neighbours cut them down. Albertine developed mildew, so I took it out and put in New Dawn, which did much better.

I gave my neighbours roses, too, to cover the white front of their shop. In three summers Golden Showers nearly climbed to their second floor. I also gave them Málaga, Danse du Feu and Wedding Day. This last was quite a tongue-twister for Robert to pronounce. It flowered together with *Clematis macropetala*, a marvellous combination.

Anemones and freesias did spendidly, and the latter's fragrance was delightful in the still, dry air. Sparaxis, tigridas, ranunculus, chincherinchees and antirrhinums flourished too. Rudbeckias were a striking addition and so were lime-green nicotianas, while Busy Lizzies flowered repeatedly in the shadier parts of the garden. We stuck straggly old geraniums from London all round the pear tree, and Martyn covered them over generously with twigs so they survived the winter to blazon forth the next year with renewed life. In between giving concerts in Holland I bought masses of tulips, and when they flowered in a regimental parade of red and yellow, the Catalan national colours, everyone in the village was gratified at what seemed to be a diplomatic gesture.

One day I was alone, eating my lunch in the sunny garden we had created, thinking happily how lucky I was to find such a heavenly spot to call my own, when the country chair I was ensconced in collapsed and I fell backwards into Parade and the pear tree.

Two wisterias, clematis and climbing roses were added, leading the ex-president of the Cave, Monsieur Chiffre, to remark: 'If there is an inch of earth bare, Madame will cover it!' Every time I arrived at La Bergerie, I had to prune and tidy up the jungle it had become, so rapidly did everything grow.

On either side of the entrance to the house I planted climbing Peace in two comportes (the old grape 'baskets'), together with *Clematis spooneri* on the left and Rouge Cardinal on the right.

The villagers were endlessly kind to me, giving me grapes or cherries in *eau de vie*, or recipes, or advice. They taught me how to make *roquette*, a delicious, frilly, herbal lettuce, sprout in twenty-four hours in the heat by sowing the seeds and covering them with an old wet sheet, kept dampened. Another tip was to sow the seeds in a wet handkerchief dipped into a cup of water.

Since the age of twelve I had spent most of my life in capital cities – Brussels, London, New York – and touring all over the world, rarely staying longer than twenty-four hours or a few days in any one place. For the last fifteen years I had been in Bruton Place, Mayfair, so it was hardly surprising that I had little knowledge of how French country people lived. My Spanish maid in London asked me: 'Why do you always live in animals' houses? Here it is horses, in France it is sheep!'

For two years I spent as much time as I could at Rasiguères anonymously. I was known simply as 'L'anglaise'.

'I don't want to leave,' I told Josette in the shop one day. 'But I must work.'

'Work?' she asked. 'What work?'

'I am a pianist,' I told her.

'Where do you play?' she demanded.

'All over the world,' I replied.

'Will you play for us one day?'

Rasiguères radically altered my view of the world. I came to know these delightfully kind and hospitable country people who worked so hard all their lives, rising at three o'clock in the summer. And should the rain not fall abundantly and at the right time, or a late frost nip the growing grapes, they would have no wine to sell and no income. They all laboured in the vineyards, with secondary industries of almonds, apricots, pears and peaches. Peaches could be bought for fifty pence a crate.

I was not able to go often to Rasiguères, so a year or more elapsed before I arranged for a piano to be transported there. I telephoned Josette at the *épicerie*. 'Has the piano arrived?' I asked.

'Yes. But it has no legs!'

'But Josette,' I exclaimed in consternation, 'they must be in a parcel.'

'No.'

'Are there any parcels you haven't opened?' I asked.

'There are cushions in one,' she said.

'Why not see what's underneath the cushions?'

The piano legs were there.

Robert probably had never seen a piano. He screwed the legs on the piano and leaned it against a wall while he went round the village looking for some strong men to lift the instrument into position.

When I next telephoned Josette, she said: 'Oh yes, you can come and play the piano immediately.'

Now their ears were assailed for several hours in the morning and again in the late afternoon by Moura Lympany practising on her baby grand piano in her Bergerie. And as they grew to like the sounds I made, so did I learn from them the secrets of their wine-making. The Midi is the largest and oldest vineyard running from the Pyrenees to the Rhône. The Carignan, Grenache and the Syrah are the chief varieties of grape grown there.

I persuaded Harrods to stock the Rasiguères wines. Sir Hugh Wontner of the Savoy sampled them and found them excellent. 'How much can I have?' he asked me.

In his autobiography, Lord Forte tells how he met Sir Hugh in Hyde Park one day, carrying a plastic bag, and asked him what it contained.

'Moura Lympany's wine,' Sir Hugh told Charles Forte. 'It's very good.'

I bought a little vineyard of my own bordered with figs and peach trees, and now I was one of the *propriétaires* of the Cave, one of the Cooperative. The villagers named one of their wines Cuvée Moura Lympany, and hung my portrait in the Cave.

When Peter Andry, chairman of EMI and now vice-president of Warners Entertainments Associates, and his wife Christine, great friends of mine, contemplated buying a house in Italy, I persuaded them to come to Rasiguères instead, and found them a house near the church. With their young family, it proved too small and confining, so they built a handsome new villa on high ground commanding a magnificent view of the mountains.

Much as I loved La Bergerie it was really too small, so I bought the Andrys' house and sold La Bergerie to Stanley and Sheila Moody, who promptly erected a plaque on the wall next to the door proclaiming that Moura Lympany, CBE, had lived there, and gave a lovely party to celebrate.

Martyn Thomas again designed the interior of my new house, with flowery fabrics everywhere. Opposite the kitchen he made out of a black hole of stone a small, cool, green-and-white dining-room. On the first floor was my bedroom, over the bed Van Gogh's *Irises*, an en suite bathroom and a balconied music-room, all in shades of blue. (The balcony had to be removed to allow the piano to be hoisted in and was then rebuilt.) The second-floor drawing-room, which now ran the full length of the house, had views over the vineyards and mountains beyond at the back and the church at the front. Yellow and orange Spanish rugs covered the ancient floorboards, while lime-green and white daisy-patterned sofas and chairs at one end gradually became persimmon-printed seats at the other. A wrought-iron gallery and stair-rail completed the airy perspective.

All hundred and fifty villagers had little or no experience of classical music. Marcelle Dornon recalls the exact spot en route from Toulouse to Rasiguères where I said to her: 'How would you like to have a music festival at Rasiguères?'

Marcelle replied: 'We don't have a restaurant!'

'But your mother is a wonderful cordon bleu cook!'

I excitedly recruited all my friends in the music world. I contacted Victoria de los Angeles and asked her if she would come and sing two songs. I had heard her sing on television in England. 'It's too far to come and sing two songs,' she replied. 'Can't I sing ten?'

This was a coup, since Rasiguères is near the border with Spain; Perpignan was once the province of the Princes of Barcelona. The villagers speak Spanish, French and Catalan.

The first festival was planned for 1981.

Manchester is said to be the musical heart of England. My grandmother Gertrude Mather had attended the Loreto Convent School there. When I went to Manchester to play the double concerto by Malcolm Williamson, Master of the Queen's Musick, at the Royal Northern College of Music, the orchestra was the Manchester Camerata. At the party afterwards, I talked to John Whibley, formerly cellist with the Hallé Orchestra and now full-time manager of the Manchester Camerata, the main employer of free-lance musicians outside London. There were speeches and to my surprise I was called upon to say a few words. I had no idea what I was going to say, but I stood up.

'You've all played so beautifully,' I said, 'how would you like to be my resident orchestra at Rasiguères, where I'm going to start a festival?'

A great shout went up. 'YES!' they cried.

The problem was, where should the concerts take place? At first we thought of the church, but it was impracticable. The long, rectangular interior of the Cave Cooperative reminded me of the long library at Blenheim Palace, where I had recently played at a charity recital. The Cave was where the work took place, it was the heart of the village and formed a natural auditorium. But what were the acoustics like? To our relief and delight they were excellent. The odour of wine was everywhere and the atmosphere vibrant. So we decided on the Cave. The festival thus became the Festival of Music and Wine.

The villagers were recruited by Marcelle and her mother to cook and serve a wonderful dinner after every evening's concert, to be eaten at long tables the length of the gallery upstairs at the Cave. Outside the rear of the Cave villagers assembled huge braziers of *sarments* – the prunings of the vines on which they grilled the meats. Fragrant cheeses were served, and the salads dressed incomparably from ancient local recipes handed down from mother to daughter for generations. And of course the wine flowed. Before, during and after the dinners and in the intervals of the concerts, the Cave shop and bar supplied a natural refreshment area, where three 'petrol-pumps' poured red, rosé and white muscat for the concert-goers.

A villager gave me her recipe for thyme soup, and this is how it is made. Put lots of thyme with crushed garlic into cold water, bring to the boil and simmer for twenty minutes. Remove the thyme and add a raw egg. It is a wonderful soup and, say the villagers, 'disinfects the stomach'. Their great speciality is the *cargolade* – grilled snails, the little grey ones which surface all over the village after a shower. The villagers sprinkle them with flour and then leave them for a fortnight. Now, after seasoning them with salt and pepper and ground thyme, they grill them over a brazier glowing with burning *sarments*, at the same time spearing a piece of bacon fat on the end of a bamboo stick and letting the boiling fat drip on each snail. They are served with an aïoli sauce and eaten with a bent nail, which is used to winkle the flesh out of the snail shell. The aïoli sauce is made the traditional way with just garlic and oil, a difficult and time-consuming operation.

They all are real cordon bleu cooks, and were so far earlier in history than the Parisians, because theirs is an ancient civilization. Another of their specialities is their orange and water-melon jam, which they also taught me to make. I make peach jam too, and add peaches to the *vin doux naturel*, the sweet wine from Rasiguères. For desserts, they serve peaches, fluffy meringue cakes, and fruit compôtes.

So it was, with great éclat, at the end of June 1981, that the Festival of Music and Wine was launched. The concert-goers were quartered in the village houses together with the musicians, who received warm hospitality at very modest charges. The village was crammed to bursting-point. Some of my more sophisticated friends were shocked by the 'Turkish' loos: a hole in the floor over which they were expected to squat, doubling as a shower. But only recently had such modern conveniences arrived in the village. A few years earlier all loos were buckets which the women carried up into the hills to empty into the soil round the vines.

Nor did the English audiences care for rabbit on the menu. However incomparably cooked, they detected it was rabbit, and it has never been served since at the concert dinners.

Two dancers from Sadlers Wells Ballet agreed to come out and dance at the festival. Marcelle and I met them at the airport and they were astounded when we drove into the village. 'Where's the opera-house?' they asked. 'Where's the gala?' Their names were Marion Tate and Carl Myers.

'That's the opera-house,' I said, indicating the Cave Co-operative. 'This is not a gala. It's a little village where we're bringing them some music.'

They were dismayed when they saw the tiny stage surrounded by huge wine-vats.

'How are we going to dance? There's no room!'

'Can't you dance upwards?'

'Could you make the stage bigger?'

'Can you double the stage?' Marcelle asked the men.

Within an hour the stage area was doubled.

'What will you dance?' I asked the dancers.

'A *pas de deux*.'

'What *pas de deux*?'

'Shostakovich's Second Concerto.'

Luckily I had the music so I could play that. 'What else?'

'Chopin.'

'OK.'

Larry Adler came to see if he could help. So he played a piece the dancers could dance to.

Then they mentioned a recording of Tchaikovsky's *Sleeping Beauty* and the *Nutcracker Suite,* to which they could dance. Had anyone got the record?

All the record shops in Perpignan were telephoned, but to no avail. We tried the shops in Estagel without any luck. Then someone knew of someone who knew of someone . . . and miraculously the record appeared.

The reader may well be surprised at the lack of preparation for the festival, which needs some explanation. That first year a dancer, married to a friend of mine, had agreed to come and dance for me (I had just done a charity performance for her). However, at the very last minute, she let me down. In desperation, I rang Sir John Tooley, the director at Covent Garden, and asked for his help. He then asked the director of the ballet to send me two dancers – the ones referred to above. They arrived on the morning of the performance, which is why we were still discussing programmes and other details at the eleventh hour. Today, the programmes are arranged well ahead of the festival and nothing is left to chance.

The following year six dancers came and danced part of *Swan Lake* round Marcelle's swimming-pool. From bravado I called out at the supper-party: 'Why don't you do a few steps on the tables as they used to do in Russia?'

They did and it was the coup of the soirée.

True to the spirit of Rasiguères the Catalan pop singer Jordi Barre took part. Dancers from the Sadlers Wells Ballet came again to dance, and every year the lovely blonde soprano Elizabeth Harwood sang. At the second festival the dazzling French pianist Cécile Ousset played, Larry Adler came again, and the poignant appearance of the blind

French pianist, Bernard D'Ascoli, who won second prize in the Leeds Piano Competition in 1981, brought tears to many eyes. This second year the French bank Crédit Agricole gave us generous sponsorship.

Ted Heath came out and conducted at one concert in 1983 and in his honour the villagers created a *cuvée*, a companion to mine: Cuvée Edward Heath. I enjoyed tremendously the challenge of finding artistes of the highest calibre, known and unknown, who came and willingly gave their services for the sheer joy of performing at Rasiguères. I was very proud of my discoveries. One was the superb violinist Peter Csaba, who had defected from his own country, Romania, and taken refuge in France. He was so outstanding a performer, with his dark intensity, good looks and emotional playing, that he was able to establish a reputation at Lyon with his own ensemble and became leader of the Lyon Opera Orchestra. Another was a virtuoso guitarist from Brazil of enormous, sunny charm: Dagoberto Linhares. He plays exquisitely with telling hesitations which, together with his un-Latin fairness and smiling grace, endear him to everybody. In 1986 there played for the first time the versatile and brilliant duettists Richard Markham and David Nettle, who literally play as one. And in 1989, to mark the sixtieth anniversary of my own début on the concert platform at Harrogate, I played again at Rasiguères and at the Royal Festival Hall the Mendelssohn Piano Concerto in G Minor.

But what has really made the festival at Rasiguères a continuing success has been the wonderful loyalty and support of the Manchester Camerata, who every year charter a coach for the thirty-six-hour journey to perform at my festival. Their superb musicianship under the direction of Anthony Hose is totally dependable, which is essential when a collection of artistes assemble from all four corners of the earth for seven days, performing difficult and different works in improvised circumstances, with very limited rehearsal time. They have never let me down in Rasiguères, and I can never thank them enough.

One of the great features of the festival has been the Saturday night cabaret, an impromptu affair following a week of serious music-making, which takes place after the last convivial dinner. In 1983 the dancers from the Sadlers Wells Ballet performed an unforgettable *pas de deux* in the darkened gallery above the Cave, while in 1989 the Camerata's principal cellist, Basil Howitt, inspired gales of laughter as he and a colleague impersonated Dagoberto Linhares and his protégé playing a duet on the same guitar.

Despite her illness, Elizabeth Harwood, beloved of all who knew her, came again, accompanied by her husband Julian Royle. She sang as beautifully as always, but one was aware of her frailty.

The villagers erected a sign in the place in front of the Cave: MANCHESTER SQUARE. And another leading to the river they named LYMPANY HIGHWAY.

A great sadness came to us on the last day of the festival in 1990 when news arrived that Elizabeth Harwood had died. Everybody loved her: her radiance, her warmth, her generosity.

'What do you want done if you die here?' the Mayor of Rasiguères asked me.

'Bury me in the cemetery and plant a vine on my grave!' I replied.

# 10

# Seven Chapels and a Garden

While I was at 44 Bruton Place a very sweet girl with long blonde hair, Esmé Bird,[1] who had trained as a pianist but was doing secretarial work, came to help me with my correspondence. One day, on my return from the country, I climbed up my rickety old pair of steps to switch on the electricity again after my absence. The electric meters in the house were awkwardly located above a sink in a corner of the garage. I climbed the steps, reached up to the switches, but since I had not placed my feet centrally on the tread, the ladder swayed and I fell over, hitting my right breast on the edge of the sink below as I fell. I said afterwards to Esmé, as I nursed my badly bruised breast: 'I hope this doesn't give me another cancer.'

A year later, in September 1983, Esmé reminded me of what I had said, for the same symptoms I had had in 1970 recurred, and back I went into the King Edward VII Hospital for a second operation. Richard Handley had retired; his successor Mr (now Sir William) Slack looked after me. There was a repeat performance: three months' convalescence, during which I endured the painful process of reusing my

[1]Esmé Bird later married the violinist Kenneth Sillito, leader of the Academy of St Martin-in-the-Fields.

right hand and arm to practise the piano. And similarly, there was a drastic drop in my income.

In 1983 I sold the lease of my house in Bruton Place to Maurice and Josephine Saatchi and moved to a flat on two floors with windows at the back opening on to a beautiful patio garden, in Lowndes Square.

To celebrate the tenth anniversary of my arrival in Rasiguères, and wishing to repay the villagers for all their kindness to me and the happiness they had brought me, I invited forty of them to come to London, at my expense. Two coaches were hired. They brought with them hundreds of snails, piles of *sarments*, huge braziers, aïoli sauce, and of course Rasiguères wine. I quartered as many as I could on sofas in my flat, and we celebrated with a great *cargolade* in the garden. Elizabeth Harwood sang and Peter Csaba played the violin. A lot of them had never been out of France in their lives and it was an amazing experience for them they have never forgotten. The morning following the *cargolade* the porter at the neighbouring block of flats asked me: 'What was all that lovely music next door last night?'

After a year in Lowndes Square, my bank manager was brutally frank. 'You are spending more than you are earning,' he told me.

'That's madness!' I exclaimed. 'It's going to stop, from *now*.'

I am a very determined woman when I make up my mind about something. I telephoned a man friend. 'Will you buy the rest of my lease?' I asked baldly.

'Yes,' he said immediately.

I went searching round the agencies for a big studio. However, now I found the estate agents did not want me on their books because I was a pianist. John Lill, for example, lives in an isolated cottage in Essex where only the birds and grazing cows may be disturbed by his practising. But isolation in the country would not be good for me. The other problem was space: a grand piano takes up a lot of room.

Eventually I found a suitable duplex apartment in Thurloe Square, jubilantly signed the lease and prepared to move in. On the next Sunday morning I telephoned my new landlord. 'I'm going to be your new tenant,' I announced gaily. 'I just wanted to say hello.'

He could hardly have been more crushing. 'I don't know you,' he began. 'I don't know anything about your morals or your finances. I only know you are a piano-player.'

I was somewhat taken aback. 'You could look me up in *Who's Who*,' I suggested mildly.

'One thing is I don't want any piano-playing,' he stated.

'I'll put the piano in the basement,' I offered.

'That won't help,' he objected. 'You'll have to sound-proof the whole place. Sound rises and will come through the window.'

I realized it was hopeless. I telephoned my lawyer and cancelled the whole thing.

Early in October 1983 I went to Paris to give a concert and the following day I had lunch with a woman friend. We told each other our troubles. Her husband had recently died and left her the responsibility of managing his properties.

'Why don't you let them?' I suggested.

'Would you like to rent a flat in Monte Carlo for a year?' she asked. The rent was only a few pounds more than the rates I was paying in Lowndes Square.

'I'll take it!' I said at once.

'Don't you want to see it?' she asked.

'No!'

It was a beautiful apartment on the Avenue Princesse Grace, at the eastern end of Monte Carlo. The night I arrived I stood on the terrace and looked out over the Mediterranean. It was magical, sea all around me, and I resolved then and there to stay.

A century ago, travellers could reach Monaco only by mule on a dusty road, or by sea. Beneath the beautiful palace built on a rock overlooking the sea runs a tunnel which was used as a shelter during the war years. The Lower, Middle and

Upper Corniches wind round in hair-raising hairpin bends through the loveliest country, linking the towns with the Riviera below. Italy shimmered in the distant sunlight. Leos love the sun, it brings out the best in them.

Prince Rainier's cousin Prince Louis de Polignac had been the president of the Société des Bains de Mer for over twenty years. I had known and loved his great-aunt Princesse Edmond de Polignac, who had been Winnaretta Singer when I attended her salon in Paris the year I won the second prize in the Ysaÿe Competition. She had founded the Singer-Polignac Foundation for the promotion of classical music and the arts. But it was Princess Grace's predecessor, the blonde American Alice Heine, Duchesse de Richelieu, who married Prince Albert I of Monaco, who made Monte Carlo a great centre of culture.

Monte Carlo brought me luck. It is like a village and I am never lonely here. Several friends of mine have settled here, and I have met most interesting people, including the novelist and composer Anthony Burgess, and Shirley Conran. But music is what matters most to me. It is work. Then I rest. I refuse most invitations.

One day, at one of the public functions, Prince Louis de Polignac approached me. 'Moura, I have a *propriété* in France. There are seven little chapels around there and they are going to sell them off as discos or galleries. They should be restored. Could we run a festival there and save them?'

'Of course!' I replied. 'I give concerts in churches in England.'

When I arrived to stay at Kerbastic, impeccably run to the tiniest detail, I exclaimed to Prince Louis: 'I do love luxury!'

Prince Louis regarded me indulgently: 'Non, Moura,' he rebuked me gently. 'Pas le luxe – le raffinement.'

He was right, of course.

I was quartered in the beautiful Bishop's Room and slept in a four-poster bed furnished with the finest hand-embroidered linen. The adjoining room was an opulently furnished salon for my use, with a grand piano for me to practise on whenever I liked. There were three grand pianos in the château, built by Prince Louis's aunt, Comtesse Marie-Blanche de Polignac, who had filled the château with music. The library possessed a priceless collection of music manuscripts and Prince Louis showed me the manuscript of two piano concertos by Poulenc.

The chapels were dotted about the village of Guidel on the Brittany coast, north of Quimper. Long, lovely beaches bordered the Atlantic where bracing breezes ruffled the sand-dunes. In the village, women still wore the traditional Breton white lace bonnets. Inland, it was farming country. Vast meadows of sunflowers grown for seed-oil nodded gold heads in the sea-salted air.

We toured the chapels. They were not completely in ruins, and when I went about them singing, the acoustics were fine. I was enthusiastic and said we must start straight away. Prince Louis, an absolute perfectionist, said 'Non!' Everything must be done properly. Arrangements must be made carefully; it would take two or three months. Nothing must be left to chance.

'I'm an artist!' I pleaded.

'You're a *fantaisiste,*' Prince Louis told me, insisting that all concerts must be well organized.

The first concerts of Le Festival des Sept Chappelles, as I suggested it should be called, were held in 1986, timed to take place in July, following the Rasiguères Festival of Music and Wine. We began with five of the chapels. Prince Louis, his brothers Prince Edmond and Prince Guy, and their two sisters, were the patrons of the festival. The performers, instead of staying in little stone houses in a Pyrenees mountain village, were royally entertained in Kerbastic on the outskirts of Guidel. The attention to the minutest detail, the perfectionism of Prince Louis, taught me so much. It was a revelation to me.

At the festival in 1990 we used all seven chapels for the first time. Christopher Underwood, the tenor, sang in his recital some of the songs Fauré, Poulenc and Ravel had composed for Prince Louis's aunts, Princesse Edmond de Polignac and Comtesse Marie-Blanche de Polignac, who bequeathed Kerbastic to her favourite nephew, Prince Louis. Audiences flocked to the village of Guidel and the seven chapels and Radio France usually broadcast excerpts from the festival.

Now that my life seemed set on a steady course, I was terribly shocked to be telephoned one day with the shattering news that Martyn Thomas was dead, killed in a car crash in Norfolk. He was not a good driver and had sat for his driving test many times before at last passing it. He was driving alone in thick fog on the way to see his mother in Lincolnshire. Stuck behind a lorry, he grew impatient to overtake it and met a Mercedes in a head-on collision. Martyn was killed outright and I went at once to Norfolk.

I had grown emotionally very dependent on Martyn. Our collaboration, for such it had been, on the transformation and decoration of Bruton Place, La Bergerie, Lowndes Square, and Impasse Rue de la Place at Rasiguères, had been a momentous one. His artistic spirit seemed to be everywhere I looked around me; he had designed every single cushion I had worked in my favourite Florentine stitch in sherbet colours. For a long time I was inconsolable. Martyn had understood me and my moods so well. I really had loved him. In the resulting mood of deep despondency I threw myself with renewed vigour into my music.

Just before I was due to go to Rasiguères for the 1983 festival, the owner of the apartment on the Avenue Princesse Grace reminded me she would be needing it again herself. So after the festival I persuaded a friend to drive me and my decorator 'mate' who had succeeded Martyn, Gordon Black, to Monte Carlo and help me find a new apartment. It was a magnificent drive along the Côte d'Azur in the sunshine towards Nice, beside the glittering sea.

I had heard of an apartment that was vacant and was

intrigued to see it. 'It's up there,' I told my friends, gesturing up to the perpendicular townscape behind us. 'Are you too tired to go and see it?'

'We don't mind in the slightest,' they said. So we walked up hundreds of steps to reach the villa, which looked delightful.

The next morning we obtained the key of the first floor and explored it. There was a spacious foyer, and beautiful views extended on all sides through large bay windows. By eleven o'clock I had signed the lease. I lived there happily for the next seven years. I was in Monaco, yet the other side of the road was France. The neighbours on the ground, second and third floors, whom I gradually came to know, told me they loved hearing me practise and play the piano. The one cloud, literally, was the plan to build two huge blocks of flats nearby.

In 1990, alas, the new owner of my apartment wanted to occupy it himself, and I had to move again. Ironically, I found my next apartment on the sixteenth floor of the high-rise building next to the villa: Château Périgord. It is a beautifully designed block, spacious, with a marble-floored garden gallery decorated with *trompe-l'oeil* trellises, roses and irises, orchids and honeysuckle. Behind me the stony landscape rises up and up, villas clinging like limpets to the rock, and in front lies the sea.

'The most important thing to play well is good health,' Uncle Tobs used to say. The night before a concert I am always in bed by eight o'clock and then I read. Sometimes it is a biography, such as the one of Horowitz, or something frivolous like *Vogue*. It is a good thing for the brain to change completely from the work it does. Sometimes I listen to great performers playing the music I am going to play the next day. Cortot said a good digestion was vital. Light reading, a good night's sleep and nourishing food on the days before a concert is best for me, and where food is concerned I let myself go: mangoes, yoghurt, filet steak, lots of butter and cream. When I eat better, I play better. Often I eat on the beautiful terrace facing the Mediterranean, basking in the sunshine, shaded from the glare by a blue-and-white striped awning. I eat very carefully on the day of the concert, just a grilled steak.

In the last century concert pianists travelled round the world in a caravan group. Their piano went with them, together with an entourage of tuners, secretaries, dressers and family. But during the war I became so used to playing on whatever instrument was available, irrespective of its condition or age, that I have grown accustomed to travelling alone. Sometimes a strange piano can be very hard work to play. After playing one day in the recording studio I was more than usually exhausted, the piano was too new and the keys far from easy to depress, so that to put any expression into the music was virtually impossible. The same was true of a piano at the Convent of Our Lady at Southam where I gave a charity recital. The dear nuns bought an expensive new piano especially for my recital and the keys were unbearably stiff and under-used.

At times, concert societies are false in their economies. They will spend thousands of pounds on advertising, new seats, equipping the bar, installing a restaurant, car-parks, foyer exhibitions, but rarely invest in a first-class piano. Recently complaints from visiting artists to one concert hall reached a climax when two concert pianists withdrew recordings of their work on the resident inferior instrument, thus forcing the management to invest £27,000 in a new piano.

I possess two pianos. The instrument in my music-room at Rasiguères once belonged to the composer Gerald Finzi, so closely connected with the Three Choirs Festival at Gloucester, where my great-grandparents lived and are buried. The second, in my apartment in Monte Carlo, is a Steinway grand piano measuring two metres twenty centimetres long. It was indescribably difficult to manoeuvre it into the apartment on the sixteenth floor of a block of thirty-four floors. A crane had to be used to hoist it up at the back of the block and through the french windows of my music-room, facing the mountains.

One of the most memorable pianos I have played was in Paris in a sumptuous apartment on the Avenue Foch owned by an American friend. It was an Erard piano and I felt I made the most gorgeous sounds ever on it playing Debussy and Chopin. Touring remoter parts of the world one risks having to use really dreadful instruments, but, happily for me, the pianos available on my recent tour of Australia and New Zealand were correctly tuned, concert standard grand pianos which were a pleasure to play. The modern cult of ancient instruments does not appeal to me at all. I am a woman of today and only modern instruments interest me, although I do find the newer Steinways are not what they were.

As I did in wartime England, I go to work on an egg: an hour and a half before a concert I have two boiled eggs (3½ minutes), bread and butter and a pot of strong tea. Sometimes I have three eggs in a day. Pianists need plenty of protein. The steaks have to be almost blue: just on and off the grill. And occasionally I help myself to a few lumps of sugar. These give me instant energy. My aunt, Sister Mary John, was a great believer in sugar: 'I could not get through the day', she told me once, 'without eight teaspoonfuls of sugar.'

The best tonic for me is a glass of my own muscat wine. It is very sweet and potent, brims with vitamins and minerals, yet has nothing added to it. But I never drink alcohol before a concert. Later at night I usually drink a mug of Horlicks. That helps me to sleep. My life is completely secluded. I cannot go out and practise. I never accept luncheon invitations. There is nothing in my life except my work and I have my reward in the wonderful notices.

I am in excellent health because I look after myself. I have had to learn to cope, otherwise I should have gone under. And I have no intention of doing so. It is surprising what a good kick in the pants every so often can do. All my life I have been so full of energy. I feel so strong now. My throat still irritates me a little, a hangover from the whooping cough.

I am far too busy to think about old age. There are not enough hours in the day for me to do all the things I want to do. In Monte Carlo there are ballets, operas, concerts; and there is a theatre in French and English. French television is very good. French radio broadcasts beautiful music all day long. There is my practising, my correspondence to attend to, my housekeeping to do. I am very happy here.

Concert-goers write to me not only about music but all sorts of things, and I try to answer every letter personally. After my *Woman's Hour* broadcast from the Beaumaris Festival on the Isle of Anglesey, the editor of that national institution wrote to me: 'Our listeners . . . have remarked particularly on your optimism and strength of purpose in overcoming cancer. Thank you for talking to us about something so personal.' I received many letters from similarly afflicted listeners.

Then the *Sunday Telegraph* colour supplement ran a feature called 'Formula for the Perfect Party' and I was included. To my surprise I received a letter from a reader claiming he possessed pieces of the same Mason's Ironstone dinner service I had and could we exchange missing pieces! Another correspondent wrote that he was interested in lady pianists with fascinating names: Monique de la Bruchollerie, Denise Lassimonne,[2] Gina Bachauer, and me. An unusual name sometimes presents problems: I am often mistakenly called Moira, and when I travel abroad I am usually asked to send a phonetic pronunciation of my name for radio and television announcers.

I am a morning person. I have always woken up early in the day, raring to go. Once at the hairdressers at 9 a.m. I was chatting and laughing away to Christian, the stylist who has

---

[2]Denise Lassimonne was the adopted daughter of Tobias Matthay.

dressed my hair for over thirty years, when another client asked him, was I drunk? 'Oh no,' replied Christian, 'Moura Lympany is always like that first thing in the morning!'

When people say I look younger every day, and that my forehead is completely unlined, I reply: 'It is all the hard work.'

My music comes first. In 1989 I celebrated my sixtieth jubilee as a concert pianist with a recital at the Royal Festival Hall. I was overwhelmed by astonishing reviews. The headlines ran: 'Queen of the Ivories', 'The Barbara Cartland of the Piano', 'The Versatile Specialist', 'Poet of the Piano', 'Cornish at Heart'. I believe I have acquired something of Clara Schumann's style: to play straight, nothing chichi, nor what I call *powdered* rubatos.

Every day I practise as I have done for over sixty years, in four one-hour sittings, to keep my fingers supple. I do stretching exercises, studies in sixths and octaves, fast scales in every key, then any difficult passages in a forthcoming programme. For the all-Chopin recital at the Royal Festival Hall in the autumn of 1989 I played the twenty-four Preludes Op. 28 and the B Minor Sonata No. 3 Op. 58. Exercises do not tire the brain. What tires the brain is playing at white-heat, at full strength, as at a concert. You cannot practise like that; there would be no reserves left for the performance. Some artists, such as the Brazilian pianist Giomar Novaes, do not practise on the day of a concert, nor the day before, in order to be absolutely fresh.

Unusually for a child prodigy, there has been no hiatus in my career, between the child and the fully fledged pianist, as often happens, because from my début I went on playing and at seventeen I was a young woman. I have been playing non-stop for sixty-two years. And today I play far less wrong notes. Before each concert when I am shattered with nerves I say to myself: 'Moura, why are you doing this? This is the last time!' And then I thank God for leaving me my hands.

There is only one thing to do with nerves and that is really to concentrate with your brain and your heart on what you are playing. You won't notice the nerves because you are busy. That is why it is so tiring, why one is so done in after a concert.

Then of course the minute it is over, and I hear the applause and the waves of admiration and yes, love of making marvellous music, overwhelm me, alone on the platform beside my piano, I feel exhilarated, rewarded. Sometimes, when I have come off the platform after a performance it takes a while for me to get my legs back, they tremble so much. I am 'high', intoxicated, and may say things I would not say normally. If the reviews are good, I am given courage to go forward to the next concert. If the reviews are bad, I make up my mind to play better the next time.

'Phenomenally clean articulation and power,' one reviewer wrote of my performance of Prokofiev's First and Second Piano Concertos and the three Rachmaninov piano concerti, recorded in the early fifties under Walter Susskind's baton and reissued by Olympia on compact disc. And years after I turned aside Walter Legge's suggestion that I record the Debussy Préludes and the Chopin *Fantaisie*, these are the two composers with whom I am now having such a success. Described as one of my 'most magical' recordings was an unpretentious collection of the short pieces and encores so dear to me. And a French pianist praised my Debussy to the skies. So I could not help thinking that if a Frenchman admires the way I play Debussy, then I must be quite good, mustn't I?

Another of my reviews read: 'Beyond the cavils of criticism and volatile fashions in interpretation, Lympany is a national institution.'

The French press headlined: *Impératrice, L'Enfant est devenue Grande Dame*. Indeed in the French newspapers I am alluded as *Dame* Moura Lympany.

In 1990 I played four times during the week-long Festival of Music and Wine at Rasiguères: the Saint-Saens Piano Concerto No.2; Beethoven's 'Emperor' Concerto, with

Edward Heath conducting; a solo recital; and a sonata with the violinist Peter Csaba. Between these concerts I flew to Worthing to play.

The French composer Maurice Ohana wrote to me: 'I cannot wait to tell you how impressive your performance is – there is superb maturity – a command of phrasing – tone far beyond the merely technical power. How heartening to find that age brings something more to admire, probably the result of a whole life of faith and meditation.'

The year 1989 was the fiftieth anniversary of the beginning of the Second World War and the start of the National Gallery concerts. At a recital to commemorate this the violinist Ida Haendel – who had also been a child prodigy – and I played in the Gallery. I played Bach and Schumann, and together we played César Franck. At another commemorative concert I played the Warsaw Concerto by Richard Addinsell. To hear the wartime music was to bring back to us, the performers, and the audience, those perilous and dramatic times.

The following year, 1990, was the fiftieth anniversary of the Battle of Britain, which I remember vividly, and Ted Heath asked me to play in Canterbury Cathedral. Rosalind Runcie, the wife of the then Archbishop of Canterbury, herself a pianist and an excellent teacher, was present. From the first-floor study of his serene old house cushioned by gracious lawns in the cathedral close at Salisbury, where he has found repose, music and spiritual strength, Ted wrote to me afterwards: 'I want to thank you again, with all my heart, for coming to play at the Gala Concert in Canterbury Cathedral in aid of the Battle of Britain Appeal. You played the Mozart Concerto most beautifully and I am sure you realised how strongly the audience expressed its appreciation. The famous guests were of course delighted that you were able to stay with them for dinner afterwards.'

'Your career seems to be taking off like a meteor!' wrote Lionel, another friend.

An old acquaintance, who was sent a video of me, described me thus: 'You went up to the stage all dressed in yellow, looking simply lovely and not a day older than 39! You really are a fantastic person, and I hope and pray that you will have the health and strength to give another recital on your 80th birthday.'

When I played Lizst's *Les Jeux d'Eau à la Villa d'Este* at the John Ogdon Memorial Concert, *The Independent* wrote: '. . . gentle and reviving with spraying arcs of notes flawlessly captured and balanced even at their softest'.

People tell me today that I make pianistic technical problems look easy, and I feel I owe it all to dear Uncle Tobs, for he made everything so simple. Often he had a way of reducing a very complicated problem to utter simplicity. His concept of piano sound was so varied and wonderful; we worked on the Debussy Préludes and achieved ethereal textures with the fingers barely touching the keys. He had a way of blending interpretation and technique so perfectly that one was scarcely aware of the distinction. He used to say that one should play no faster than one can think. I am constantly reminded of the wisdom of his advice.

Myra Hess, Nina Milkina, Eileen Joyce, Harriet Cohen, Irene Scharrer, Clifford Curzon and I all studied with Uncle Tobs, but we were very different from one another. To quote from the *Matthay Association Journal*: 'Instead of imbibing or producing a predictable conformity, [our] Matthay training has liberated the musical psyche of each to speak on its own terms.'

If I have a regret about the direction my career has taken, it would be that I have not played more chamber music. This was largely because I had such an early success in the solo repertoire that it took all my time. At Rasiguères I began to work with the marvellous violinist Peter Csaba, who now lives in Lyon. We played the César Franck Sonata together and I hope to do more in the future. In 1992 I am going to the Gstaad Festival and shall be playing with my colleague and contemporary Yehudi Menuhin – we are exactly the same age. And at the 1991 Promenade Concerts I shall be playing again the Mendelssohn Piano Concerto in G Minor.

In addition to performing I have begun to think in terms of doing some more extensive teaching in the future. People say to me that it is extraordinary that I should be one of the last prominent Matthay pupils who uses the Matthay principles so extensively in my work, and yet I have done so little about trying to propagate these ideas to others. I have made a start. In August 1990 a charming twenty-eight-year-old Danish-American, Ken Johanssen, was sent to me as a pupil by my old friend J.G. Links. Ken flew to Perpignan from Dallas – *Dallas* is one of my favourite television programmes and I try never to miss an episode. But Ken represents a different aspect of that famous city, which has a very strong classical music tradition. His piano tutor in Texas was Alain Naudé, who had been a pupil of Dinu Lipatti and Nadia Boulanger, and a professor of music at Cape Town University. When I was sent a tape of Ken Johanssen's playing I felt that here was a young man I could help, and I rarely, if ever, give lessons, feeling that the vocation for teaching was never part of my nature. Every day for fourteen days Ken came to me for one to two hours and together we worked on the Schumann *Fantaisie* and the First Piano Concerto by Chopin. When I told my friend in Rasiguères, Marie-Rose Foussat, that I was giving lessons to a young man aged twenty-eight, she gave me an old-fashioned look. 'Lessons in what?' she demanded sceptically.

'He's learned more in fourteen days than in five years,' observed Ken's tutor Alain Naudé, who assured me a new career as a teacher could be mine for the asking, but a friend for whom I have great respect, countered: 'You are a performer. Why should you teach? Every time you play, it is a lesson.'

But now a new idea is taking shape in my mind, the Moura Lympany School of Piano Playing. The problem is: should it be in Brittany or Roussillon? Or even Monte Carlo?

For the 1990 Festival at Rasiguères, the village revived an ancient ceremony, initiated in the year 900 by Wilfred le

Velu, Count of Catalonia, the remains of whose château, Trémoine, is the tower atop a mountain and the landmark whose image dominates the village, valley and surrounding country, and adorns all the wine labels. Ted Heath, myself, the secretary-general of the Prefecture, Monsieur Henri Ferral, the president of the bank Crédit Agricole, Monsieur Camot, and the deputy of circumscription, Monsieur Pierre Estêve, were all enthroned as Companions of Trémoine. We were decorated with specially struck silver medals hung on red ribbons by the officers of the Cave Cooperative in their traditional costume of red berets and black aprons, and presented with ceremonial gifts: Ted Heath with a pair of secateurs, Monsieur Camot with a rake, and I with a pair of *souffleurs* – very useful for the open fire in the kitchen of my house at Rasiguères. Present at the ceremony was Emil Gazeu, recently retired directeur of la Cave Cooperative, a post he held for forty years. The presentations were made by dear Paul Chiffre, the oldest Companion of Wine in the village, a grand maître aged eighty-three, an old soldier who spent four long years as a prisoner of war of the Nazis in one of the Stalags. My nephew Christopher Johnstone flew from New Zealand, where he is now the director of the National Gallery at Auckland, so we had a happy reunion together with his lovely girl-friend Louise, now his wife.

I was so proud that the grand maître of French music came and played at Rasiguères: Jean Françaix, whose first compositions were published when he was twelve years old, whose music is elegant and gloriously witty. He had been a protégé of Nadia Boulanger and Princesse de Polignac. Maître Françaix asked me afterwards: was my spontaneity studied? Spontaneity comes from incessant study! I know in my head what I want the music to sound like and, at the moment of playing, it should emerge replete with my feeling and passion. Every time I play the Chopin Waltz it sounds different, according to how I feel at the time.

'More than anything, I must have flowers, always, always,' said Claude Monet. Gardening has been one of my great passions. As I have said, I gardened at my house in Surrey during the war, and at Long Island; I made a lovely roof garden at Bruton Place, and created another garden at La Bergerie. I have a terrace now in my flat at Château Périgord, but at Impasse Rue de la Place only a few pots outside the front door. When I have needed to, I could go up to 'the apricots' – a small area beside the road that came with the Andrys' house. There were two apricot trees and a fig tree and just room to swing my hammock. Martyn and I planted over fifty roses round the patch. It was fun, unkempt, wild and convenient, but it was not enough.

From the first moment I set foot in Rasiguères I had been fascinated by the awe-inspiring valley of Trémoine, abandoned some years earlier by the miners whose livelihood stemmed from digging up the red iron-ore in the soil which, as I said, gives the region its name. Dwellings and workshops had been built there. Along the river-bed, now dry, there are at least three grottoes, natural underground passages explored and mapped by local palaeontologists, wearing hard hats with a gas-lamp on the front. More recent owners had been a Catalan market gardener and his family who had built a greenhouse and installed electricity and water but had found it not viable as a commercial proposition. The valley was beautiful, ringed with mountains, and I felt it could be cultivated and made productive again. So when the opportunity arose to buy the land, I could not resist it. I did not quibble or haggle but paid the asking price. My vision was largely unplanned; I just thought of making a garden, and wondered if perhaps in time the stone houses could be restored. It was an absurd, huge, Quixotic project, but help has come from others who share my enthusiasm.

Once I had made the pilgrimage to Giverny, the garden Monet created in Normandy round his rose-pink and green-shuttered farmhouse. I love his paintings and especially the works which he painted in his garden, created by him especially for that purpose. Of course I had not his family, who helped him, or the six gardeners who ultimately gardened for him, or his genius as an artist. But I was inspired by Monet to create my own version of his visionary garden, in Roussillon.

The chief feature at Giverny is La Grande Allée, an avenue of wide, low arches over which climb varieties of old roses, the ground below carpeted with nasturtiums. Then because I love exotic plants and as I already had a temperature-controlled plant nursery, I established hibiscus, *Gloriosa superba*, strelitzia, bananas and other tropical plants. Round and about I planted my favourite *Lagerstroemia*, tree hibiscus, carnations, buddleia, fig trees and fuchsias; mimosa and cherry; zinnias, dahlias, petunias, heartsease, pansies and black-eyed Susans. A multitude of seeds I scattered everywhere. The Mediterranean temperatures dictate what will and what will not survive in the ground.

It is a twenty-five-minute winding walk from the village with bends that take nerves to drive round. Some of my friends cannot face the terrifying drive on the unmade-up road.

Jean-Marie, the potter, who with his wife established a pottery in the village, was tremendously interested in what I was doing at Trémoine; the garden and the hothouse. The house had to be temperature-and-humidity controlled and the surrounding plants had to be watered regularly. Jean-Marie organized the whole thing and installed machinery, pumps, automatic spraying. 'You're my manager,' I told him.

In 1989 I spent the hottest month of the year, August, working every day all day at my valley and I found on my return to Monte Carlo that my fingers had seized up and I could not play the piano at all. It took me three weeks to play again.

I love it here in Monte Carlo, where the sun shines most of the time and I have beautiful views from all my windows. I am making my terrace into a bower, with bougainvillaea, clematis, roses, jasmine, passion-flowers, geraniums and hibiscus. The country itself is smaller than Central Park in New York, and safer, for it has more policemen per person than anywhere else in the world. Uniformed in black and navy blue with white hats and gloves, they are everywhere. Provided foreign residents can maintain their financial independence, they are made welcome and are free of taxes.

My wonderful Italian housekeeper is a fabulous cook whose late husband was chef at the Hôtel de Paris. No matter what she cooks, it tastes better from her hands than anyone else's. She cossets me, tells me to go to bed, and will then bring me a tray. She is a worker – just like I am at the piano.

When Rostropovich came to play in Monte Carlo he told me an anecdote that took me back fifty years to the time when I was twenty-one and competed in the Ysaÿe Competition in Brussels. Rostro had been playing in Russia and had met Jacob Flier who, suffering an injury to one of his hands, had made a career as a teacher. He spoke to Rostro about me. 'You know that little English girl,' he said. 'She beat me!' And he confessed he had fallen a little bit in love with me.

I was very touched by this story. 'D'you know, Rostro,' I said, amazed, 'I was a little bit in love with him!'

So I look to the future of more concerts, directing and developing the two festivals at Rasiguères and Guidel, and always in the back of my mind is the growing garden at Trémoine. I am away for much of the year, and so when at last I reach Rasiguères it is always a great surprise to see how it has changed and matured. I have apricot trees there and figs, and I am always sad when I have to leave before the fruit is ripe and I am unable to make the jams

I love to make. My friends say that I could earn my living making apricot and fig jam, because they are so good – and no wonder, since I pick the fruit in the morning and make the jam in the afternoon! Every time I revisit my valley at Trémoine, I discover something new. These seeds have sprouted and leapt into fervent life, others have dried up and rotted beneath the ground. It is a never-ending joy to me to spend a day or take a picnic supper to Trémoine and, after gardening with my friends, to eat and drink, talk and laugh till night falls and we can breathe in the scented air, gaze at the stars in the sky and listen to the nightingales.

# Concerto Repertoire

| | |
|---|---|
| Jean Absil | Concerto |
| Richard Arnell | Concerto |
| J.S. Bach | D minor |
| Beethoven | Nos 1, 2, 3, 4, 5 |
| Lennox Berkeley | Concerto for 2 pianos |
| Bloch | Concerto Grosso |
| | Scherzo Fantasque |
| Brahms | Nos 1, 2 |
| Chopin | No. 2 F minor |
| Debussy | Fantasy |
| de Falla | Nights in the Gardens of Spain |
| Delius | Concerto |
| D'Indy | Symphonie Montagnarde |
| Dohnanyi | Variations on a Nursery Theme |
| César Franck | Symphonic Variations |
| Armstrong Gibbs | Peacock Pie Suite |
| Edvard Grieg | A minor |
| Joseph Haydn | D major |
| John Ireland | Concerto |
| Khachaturian | Concerto |
| Litolff | Scherzo from Concerto Symphonique No. 4 |
| Tobias Matthay | Concert Piece |
| Mendelssohn | Concerto in G minor |
| | Capriccio Brilliante |
| | Rondo Brilliante |

| | |
|---|---|
| Mozart | A major, K 414 |
| | B flat major, K 456 |
| | C major, K 467 |
| | C minor, K 491 |
| Paderewski | Concerto |
| | Fantaisie-Polonaise |
| Poulenc | Aubade |
| Prokofiev | Nos 1, 3 |
| | No. 4 for left hand |
| Rachmaninov | Nos 1, 2, 3, 4 |
| | Variations on a Theme of Paganini |
| Ravel | Concerto |
| | Concerto for left hand |
| Alan Rawsthorne | Concerto No. 1 |
| Saint-Saens | Concerto in G minor |
| | Wedding Cake Waltz |
| Schumann | Concerto in A minor |
| | Concertstück |
| Cyril Scott | Concerto |
| Scriabin | Concerto |
| Shostakovich | Concerto No. 2 |
| Tchaikovsky | No. 1 in B flat |
| | Fantasy |
| Turina | Rapsodia Sinfónica |
| Weber | Konzertstück |
| Malcolm Williamson | Nos 2, 3 and Concerto for 2 pianos |

# *Index*